JOHN DEERING AND MARTINA Y. FEILZER

PRIVATISING PROBATION

Is Transforming Rehabilitation the
End of the Probation Ideal?

SHORTS POLICY & PRACTICE

First published in Great Britain in 2015 by

Policy Press
University of Bristol
1-9 Old Park Hill
Bristol
BS2 8BB
UK
t: +44 (0)117 954 5940
pp-info@bristol.ac.uk
www.policypress.co.uk

North America office:
Policy Press
c/o The University of Chicago Press
1427 East 60th Street
Chicago, IL 60637, USA
t: +1 773 702 7700
f: +1 773 702 9756
sales@press.uchicago.edu
www.press.uchicago.edu

© Policy Press 2015

British Library Cataloguing in Publication Data
A catalogue record for this book is available from the British Library.

Library of Congress Cataloging-in-Publication Data
A catalog record for this book has been requested.

ISBN 978-1-4473-2728-8 (paperback)
ISBN 978-1-4473-2730-1 (ePub)
ISBN 978-1-4473-2731-8 (Mobi)

The rights of John Deering and Martina Y. Feilzer to be identified as the authors of this work has been asserted by them in accordance with the Copyright, Designs and Patents Act 1988.

Cover design by Andrew Corbett
Front cover: image kindly supplied by Getty

Contents

Acknowledgements   v

1 **Introduction**   1
   Introduction   1
   The study   4
   A brief history of the present   7

2 **Respondent views on the purposes and values of the Probation Service**   15
   Introduction   15
   Joining the Probation Service   16
   Does the Probation Service have an underpinning agreed set   22
   of values?
   Are probation values under pressure?   30
   A dividing service – management and practitioners at odds?   34

3 **Is this the end of an ideal?**   39
   Has the service lived up to expectations?   39
   If 'values' are 'in decline', why might this be?   48
   What should be the job of the Probation Service?   53

4 **Prospects for the future**   61
   Protecting the legacy of probation – the new National Probation   61
   Service
   Collaboration between the National Probation Service and Community   69
   Rehabilitation Companies – mending a broken relationship?
   If you could change the world ...   78
   Perspectives on legitimacy – who should do 'probation work'?   82

5	Subsequent events – reflecting on institutional change as it happens, further discussion and conclusion	95
	Developments since June 2014 – reflecting on institutional change as it happens	95
	Possible futures for probation work?	97
	Final comments and conclusion	101

References	105

Appendices	115
1: Full tables of survey attitudinal data	116
2: Respondent demographics	127
3: The full survey	129

Index	145

Acknowledgements

We owe a great debt to all probation staff who took the time to respond to our survey during a turbulent time. We appreciate how difficult it would have been to respond to questions about an issue that, for many, was emotionally charged. We are enormously grateful for the detailed comments provided and hope that our account is a fair reflection of our respondents' concerns and thoughts.

We are also grateful to Napo and the Probation Trusts, who circulated our survey, and to the editorial team at Policy Press, who have been supportive and incredibly efficient, allowing us to publish this report in a timely manner.

Some of the material used in this report was previously published in the *Probation Journal* as Deering, J., Feilzer, M. and Holmes, T. (2014) 'The transition from public to private in probation – values and attitudes of managers in the private sector', *Probation Journal*, 61(3): 234–50. We are grateful to the editors of the *Probation Journal* for permission to use this material.

1

INTRODUCTION

Introduction

The year 2014 brought an unprecedented challenge to the Probation Service and its staff. After over 100 years of work as a public sector organisation, the Probation Service no longer exists as a unified public body. There have been perceived threats to the institution and governance of probation in the past and many changes over the past 20 years that have been aimed at controlling probation from the centre. One of the main reasons for this was successive governments' desire to change probation values perceived to be too soft on crime and thereby to try to change practitioner behaviour, as well as to attract a new 'type' of person into the profession. Probation staff values appeared to survive previous threats but the current challenges threaten 100 years of development of an ideal around probation as a public sector endeavour.

This study is based upon research conducted with over 1,300 Probation Service employees in March and April 2014, that is, before the division (on 1 June 2014) of the Probation Service for England and Wales into a new National Probation Service (NPS – part of the civil service) and 21 Community Rehabilitation Companies (CRCs). CRCs were initially wholly state-owned organisations but were subsequently transferred to private and third sector ownership in February 2015. The study also draws on findings from a small-scale, qualitative pilot study with probation managers who had moved to the private sector (for a full discussion of this research, see Deering et al, 2014). The current study took place in March/April 2014, and participants completed an online questionnaire that elicited both qualitative and quantitative responses to a range of questions about why they had joined the service, its values and what its role should be, before considering the prospects for marketisation and privatisation under 'Transforming Rehabilitation' (TR) (Ministry of Justice, 2013).

While the views expressed were wide-ranging, a strong underlying trend was normative, encapsulating the 'probation ideal': a public sector, constructive, humanistic approach to community supervision that did not include the making of profit from punishment and thus, indirectly, from the commission of crime itself. As a result, we have grouped responses such that the analysis is focused upon this ideal of probation as a public sector endeavour.

At this point, we want to draw a distinction between the ideal of probation as a public sector endeavour and rehabilitation as defined by government as a purpose of sentencing. Clearly, the old Probation Service performed many functions beyond rehabilitation, particularly in recent decades given the emergence of punishment in the community, protection of the public and risk assessment and management. Additionally, probation served as a reminder of the inherent worth and rights of the people it worked with beyond their status as offenders. Thus, while some or all of probation's functions could survive the TR changes *in some form*, the probation ideal is in danger of being lost. In this text, we consider the ways and extent to which probation, its functions and its ideal might change and what, if anything, might remain of the probation ideal in the future. For the purposes of this study, we would define the probation ideal as a public sector task that aims to engage with those under its supervision in a humanistic and supportive manner with a view to encouraging behavioural change, while recognising structural and social disadvantage as important factors in offending that need to be addressed.[1]

The Probation Service's methods of engagement developed and varied throughout its history, and, in our view, tended to be underpinned by an individual relationship between supervisor and supervisee that was based on: respect for the individual; a non-judgemental approach; a belief in the individual's ability to change; a balance between 'care and control' (to more recently include risk and public protection); pro-social modelling; and an appreciation that crime had its roots in a complex mix of social causes and individual factors unique to the individual. Furthermore, we would argue that methods of engagement contained an element of a rights-based promise to the offender (as a citizen) to provide legitimate social opportunities (Robinson, 2008: 431). Thus, methods of intervention and/or support were perceived as needs- and rights-based and not focused on any notion of punishment. The research reported upon here considers this definition and tries to evaluate from probation staff's perspective how much of it can survive current and forthcoming TR changes.

Thus, while rehabilitation is part and parcel of the world of probation, probation practice and discourse tend to be wider than rehabilitation alone. In drawing a distinction with rehabilitation, we acknowledge that it can have a number of nuanced meanings and that the term has mushroomed and been used in various ways. For example, Robinson (2008: 430) discusses the evolution of rehabilitation according to three dominant contemporary penal narratives, namely, utilitarian, managerial and expressive rehabilitation.

In Robinson's terms, we would argue that government has come to define rehabilitation narrowly as utilitarian, synonymous with reducing reoffending. Moreover, in the context of probation, rehabilitation is constructed as expert support for the 'less than fully responsible individual' offender (Ashworth and Roberts, 2012: 869). In this sense, it could encompass a wide range of interventions with individuals, provided that these are effective in terms of reduced reoffending, in other words, whatever 'gets the job done'. TR explicitly proposes to 'tailor rehabilitative work, with an emphasis on responding to the *broader life management issues* that often lead offenders back to crime' (Ministry of Justice, 2013: 6, emphasis added). It is thus a much narrower notion than that of 'probation work' outlined earlier. Not only that, but it is also politically and philosophically different in that the government model (in our view) is very much about 'fixing what is wrong' with the individual, for example: anti-social attitudes, poor thinking skills, drug and/or alcohol misuse, homelessness, and so on. In this way, it emphasises personal responsibility, and where it does acknowledge aspects of socio-economic disadvantage, it looks to address these at an individual rather than structural level.

The study

The Probation Workers' Views of 'Transforming Rehabilitation' survey was conducted online in the spring of 2014. The aim was to survey probation staff on their views of TR; however, there is no public record or list of probation staff that could have been used as a sampling frame. Thus, in order to gain access to probation staff and to maximise the number of responses, Napo[2] and 28 of the Probation Trusts in England and Wales[3] were approached and asked if they would make the URL link to the survey available to all probation employees. Neither Napo nor the Probation Trusts were asked to comment upon or endorse the survey, but to act as a conduit to staff. Napo agreed to disseminate the survey to its members. The response from Probation Trusts was varied, many did not respond to the query but some did pass on the survey URL to staff. We received a small number of responses from Probation Trusts indicating unwillingness to disseminate our survey due to its perceived politically sensitive nature. In the debate during the early days of TR, Probation Trusts leadership had been notably quiet and the unwillingness of some Probation Trusts to pass on the information about our survey perhaps highlights the political pressure that they were under.

In the event, the overwhelming majority of respondents (n = 1,222; 94.4%) received the questionnaire via Napo, while 72 (5.6%) received it via a Probation Trust. A total of 1,311 probation employees took part in the survey (17 respondents did not indicate how they had gained access to the survey). The research population was all probation staff but there is little demographic information on this group that would allow us to test whether our respondents were representative of the wider population. All probation staff should have access to Internet services and the survey was sent via trade union or Probation Trust email lists. Importantly, our respondents chose whether or not to respond to the survey and, as a result, this is a self-selecting sample and so cannot be taken as a representative sample of probation staff.

Most respondents indicated that they had received the survey through Napo and it seems likely that this pattern of responses has skewed the results. Additionally, the survey suffered from a non-response error – namely, it is likely that those who did not respond differ from our respondents in some relevant details (Schonlau et al, 2009: 293). A lack of comprehensive information about the demographic profile of probation staff means that it was impossible to weight survey responses. In any event, we do not make claims at representativeness, nor did we set out to produce results that we could generalise to all probation staff. The aim of the survey was to explore probation staff views regarding the impact of TR on probation values and practices, and we rate highly the detailed qualitative commentary of our respondents. The size of the sample represents some 10% of probation employees.[4] In light of numerous protests against the TR changes, national strikes over privatisation in November 2013 (BBC, 2013)[5] and March 2014, and forceful objections from some interest groups such as the Howard League, it is reasonable to conclude that the views expressed in the survey represent a significant level of opinion within the Probation Service in 2014. Finally, previous research has highlighted the surprisingly homogeneous probation practice culture (see Deering, 2011; Mawby and Worrall, 2011; Robinson et al, 2014), and we are confident that views expressed in relation to questions of probation values, reasons for joining and so on are similar to those found in previous research. Thus, our sample did not appear to be anomalous.

Our survey respondents were interesting in terms of some of their key features: 65% of the sample were female[6] and only 13% had worked for the service for fewer than seven years; 67% had been in the service for over 10 years. The gender balance is similar to that of the service overall (Annison, 2013: 50), but the balance in relation to the length of service indicates that these issues are perhaps regarded as more pressing by longer-serving staff or that perhaps more longer-serving staff are members of Napo. In terms of grades, some 53% of respondents were probation officers and 23% were Probation Service officers, the remaining respondents being of managerial and case administration grades. Our sample included a slightly higher proportion of probation managers (15%) than is present in probation staff nationally (10%) (Ministry of Justice, 2014a). Finally, 31% were qualified under the Diploma in Probation Studies, some 24% were qualified or qualifying under the Probation Qualifications Framework, and some 15% had the Certificate of Qualification in Social Work.

One of the striking features of the survey is the homogeneity of responses, despite the varied nature of the sample as a whole. This is covered in detail later, but the number of statistically significantly differences between subgroups, divided by gender, grade, age and so on was small, being limited to different perceptions of the level to which probation was underpinned by agreed values, a perception that offender supervision needed to be more flexible and other small differences set out later.

The full text of the survey and data tables are included in Appendices 1–3. The survey consisted of a number of closed questions with open comments sections, open questions, and Likert attitudinal statements. Quantitative data were analysed using SPSS [Statistical Package for the Social Sciences] and qualitative data were analysed using an initial 'cloud' analysis, followed by the use of NVivo for more detailed thematic analysis. Cloud analysis uses a simple technique of counting the number of times that words and short phrases are used by respondents and presents these as percentages, that is, the percentage of respondents who included these words and phrases. This can be seen to be a somewhat crude tool, but it is one that does allow themes to emerge from the data for further in-depth analysis through the use of NVivo.

A brief history of the present

In order to put the survey in context, it is necessary to outline some of the events preceding the publication of the reform strategy *Transforming Rehabilitation* (Ministry of Justice, 2013), without revisiting the history of the Probation Service in detail (this has been done elsewhere, eg, Vanstone, 2004; Canton, 2011). Following the Probation of Offenders Act 1907, the service developed and grew in terms of its workload, level of training, expertise and influence. It widened its scope from the informal supervision by police court 'missionaries' focused on controlling probationers' alcohol misuse but it took another two decades for probation services to be provided by professionals everywhere across England and Wales (Raynor, 2012: 931). In terms of its direction and practice, probation was largely independent of central government until the *Statement of national objectives and priorities* (Home Office, 1984) began the process of increasing central control, which was influenced by the so-called 'death of rehabilitation' within the era of 'nothing works' (Lipton et al, 1975). Scepticism over the philosophical and moral argument for the treatment approach (Bottoms and McWilliams, 1979; Raynor, 2012: 932) supported the government's view that the service should move away from a generalised rehabilitative ideal to one emphasising alternatives to custody (Raynor and Vanstone, 2002). While retaining a commitment to rehabilitation, the Criminal Justice Act 1991 was famously intended to bring the service 'centre stage' as part of Home Secretary Douglas Hurd's intention to reduce the use of custody in a new era of just deserts (Raynor, 2012: 935). Alongside this came a move to control probation practice and move it in the direction of offender management, punishment and public protection via the first in a series of National Standards documents, which set out how often individuals needed to report under the terms of probation and community service orders and prescribed breach proceedings should they fail to do so (Home Office, 1992). In this way, the probation order, a new sentence of the court, became part of 'punishment in the community'. Alongside this, the emergence of 'what works' (McGuire, 2001) and the 'rise of risk' (Kemshall, 2003) added complexity to the changing face of probation practice through the 1990s. Importantly, these policy changes set the scene for a gradual move away from the one-to-one relationship between the probation officer and the offender as the prime focus for 'offending work' to a focus on referring offenders to accredited programmes and, eventually, to offender management.

While the Conservative government continued to focus on more managerialist themes and considered merging probation and prisons and even abolishing probation's supervisory function (Home Office, 1995, 1996), it was the election of the Labour government in 1997 that presaged the most radical change to probation governance when it created the National Probation Service for England and Wales. The new service's priorities (Home Office, 2001) ranked 'rehabilitation' as the fifth of five, those placed above stressing the reduction of reoffending, the protection of the public, the punishment of offenders and the need to confront offenders with the impact of crime on victims. The clear aim of the government was to control the service and move practitioners' behaviour in its favoured direction – towards punishment in the community, public protection and the reduction of reoffending – but it is unclear to what degree practitioners' underlying values and behaviour were influenced. There is evidence to suggest that while not immune to government changes, their motivations and practice remained in some ways closer to more traditional, individualised needs-based approaches, and individuals continued to join the service for traditional reasons, seeing the job as primarily broadly rehabilitative and supportive of individual needs (Williams, 1995; Vanstone, 2004; Annison et al, 2008; Deering, 2010, 2011; Mawby and Worrall, 2013). Moreover, it may well be that practitioners resisted the imposed changes by 'adaptively and strategically interpreting, evaluating, [and] reconstructing' central priorities (Cheliotis, 2006: 324), acknowledging differences between corporate and practitioner views of quality service provision and remaining true to their perceptions of quality service provision (Robinson et al, 2014: 135).

Within only a few years of the national service's creation, the desire of the government to open up probation work to competition via the marketisation of its functions became evident when it commissioned the Carter Report – *Managing offenders, reducing crime: the correctional services review* (Carter, 2003). This recommended the effective abolition of the service as a separate entity within the criminal justice system via absorption into the new National Offender Management Service (NOMS) (Burke and Collett, 2010: 236). NOMS was created administratively in 2004 to oversee the work of both the probation and prison services. However, its longer-term purpose was to introduce the market into probation work by proposing a purchaser–provider split, with NOMS commissioning 'probation services' initially from new, semi-autonomous Probation Trusts, but later from potentially any public, private or voluntary body (Carter, 2003). After a number of different proposals and models, the Offender Management Act 2007 finally created the conditions for a privatised, market-led system by requiring only limited services to courts to be provided by probation and allowing all other functions to be commissioned by the secretary of state from 'any other person' (Ministry of Justice, 2011: para 25). However, in the short term, probation's role was protected until 2010 (Straw, 2007). Nevertheless, the Labour government effectively started the process of privatisation of probation practice that culminated in the split between the NPS and CRCs.

With the election of the Coalition government in 2010, Justice Minister Kenneth Clarke signalled what appeared to be a more liberal approach to criminal justice by announcing a 'rehabilitation revolution', addressing what he referred to as the 'revolving door' of repeated reoffending, particularly of ex-prisoners (Clarke, 2010). He wished to see a reduction in the use of 'ineffective' short prison sentences and their replacement by 'effective' community sentences. However, while this might be seen at first as a liberalisation of sentencing, a closer look at the details of the proposals signalled a significant escalation of Labour's policy of the marketisation of probation work. These plans were fully realised in May 2013, when the government published *Transforming Rehabilitation* (Ministry of Justice, 2013) and announced its intention to press ahead with the marketisation and privatisation of some 70% of probation functions by 2015.

The changes proposed within TR were made possible by the Offender Management Act 2007. Other proposals, namely, the compulsory post-custody supervision of short-term prisoners, were enacted via the Offender Rehabilitation Act 2014. Although controversial and strongly opposed by the probation trade union and professional association (Napo, 2013), the government pressed ahead with TR. The National Probation Service for England and Wales, created in 2001, came to an end on 1 June 2014, succeeded by a new NPS and 21 new CRCs.

The TR document divided its proposals for the new system into three main areas: reducing reoffending (Ministry of Justice, 2013: 9–19); protecting the public (Ministry of Justice, 2013: 20–3); and making the system work (Ministry of Justice, 2013: 24–32). The changes to supervision were intended to be cost-neutral, including the large increase in numbers being supervised as a result of post-custody supervision for short-term prisoners. TR simply declared that this would be achieved by 'competing the majority of services' and a 'more efficient public sector service' (Ministry of Justice, 2013: 11), but no further details were given. It further stated that all risk assessments of offenders coming before the courts would be carried out by the NPS, initially for court reports and thereafter to decide whether individuals would be supervised by the NPS or a CRC. In terms of the CRCs, commissioning structures were intended to provide a mix of providers responsive to local needs, but no detail was given about the requirements of staff expertise in the future. The NPS would be expected to employ professionally trained probation staff; the CRCs, however, would only be expected to provide a workforce with (unspecified) 'appropriate levels of training and competence' (Ministry of Justice, 2013: 26). An important element of the commissioning structure was the introduction of Payment by Results (PbR) to 'incentivise providers to reduce offending by combining "fee for service" elements ... with "payment by results" elements linked to success', under which private/voluntary service providers would be paid only if they delivered on agreed results (Ministry of Justice, 2014b: 14). In the event, the PbR element was restricted to one element, namely, reducing reoffending (Ministry of Justice, 2014b), and the emphasis on PbR was significantly reduced, making this more of a 'traditional' privatisation more attractive to bidders. At the time of writing (January/February 2015), the percentage of the contract dependent upon PbR was unknown.

Setting up the new probation governance raised questions of continuity of employment, and in May 2014, staff were transferred to the CRCs through a statutory Staff Transfer Scheme that offered a number of protections, namely: protection from compulsory redundancy for seven months post-CRC share sale; a transfer scheme that protected the terms and conditions of employment on transfer; and the establishment of role boundaries and pay banding (NNC, 2014: D3/2–5). Additionally, CRCs and the NPS adopted the existing pay and conditions of service agreements for staff, and protected pay would be available for a period of three years (NNC, 2014: D3/6). Nevertheless, our respondents were clearly worried about being transferred to the private sector, where employment protection and pay were felt to lie below those in the public sector in many cases. For example, in the Prison Service in 2011, the salary for a typical private sector prison officer was recorded as being some £6,000 less than their public sector counterpart (Hansard, 2011). Throughout the evolution of TR, Napo has expressed its members' concerns over career progression, reductions in staff and pay (see, eg, Napo, 2014).

At the time of writing (January/February 2015), successful bids for the 21 CRCs had been announced, and ownership was transferred in February 2015. The NPS is split into seven divisions, but its divisions and CRC areas are not coterminous. Ownership structures in the 21 CRCs are complicated, as shown by the overview in Table 1.1. It is clear that private sector companies have secured the 'prime contractor' status in the majority of CRCs, but there are also interesting partnership arrangements involving social enterprises, a probation staff mutual and third sector charities. This diversity of arrangements questions the notion of a private sector takeover, as well as presuming a particular management style. On the other hand, it raises concerns as to how various CRCs will be governed and the potential for existing, different, regional and local probation cultures to deepen.

Thus, while changes introduced by previous governments sought to change the occupational culture of probation staff, the current set-up changes the delivery of community sentences and the supervision of offenders released from prison at a structural and organisational level, raising questions of legitimacy and responsibility. Critics of the new arrangements have argued the fundamental point that profit should not be made from punishment (and thus indirectly from crime itself) and that the state alone should be responsible for the punishment of offenders (for a discussion, see Genders, 2002). Furthermore, it has been argued that the changes introduced are a result of political ideology, in that there is no empirical evidence to support the claims that the changes will prove more effective in reducing reoffending (Burke, 2013; Napo, 2013). In a similar vein, Burke (2013) states that the government has chosen to ignore evidence of probation effectiveness based upon an effective professional relationship between supervisor and offender (NOMS, 2013a), and further argues that this relationship will be placed at risk by the inevitable fragmentation of supervision under the set-up of the NPS and CRCs. Supervision within the CRCs may involve intervention from a number of agencies, something that has been argued for some time as inimical to effective practice and building relationships that support processes of desistance (Raynor and Maguire, 2006; Maguire and Raynor, 2010; Raynor et al, 2013). Table 1.1 provides an early indication of the complexity introduced into probation structures and governance. The organisational structures of the CRCs vary and this may impact on their organisational priorities and future practice.

Interpretation of the proposed changes at a penal theory level has been mixed, with some commentators suggesting that they reflect an increasing form of consumerism in criminal justice policy regarding the delivery of effective and risk-reducing justice as a commodity (Crook and Wood, 2014). Others argue that TR represents a continuation of the risk management approach ultimately benefiting the private 'security–industrial complex' of global security operations (Fitzgibbon

Table 1.1: Ownership arrangements for Community Rehabilitation Companies in 2014

CRC owner	No of CRCs owned	Regions	Sector
Sodexo Justice Services in partnership with Nacro	6	Cumbria & Lancashire; Northumbria; South Yorkshire; Bedfordshire, Northamptonshire, Cambridgeshire & Hertfordshire; Norfolk & Suffolk; Essex	Private sector lead with third sector involvement
Purple Futures: Interserve in partnership with 3SC, Addaction, P3, Shelter	5	Cheshire & Gt Manchester; Hampshire & Isle of Wight; Humberside, Lincolnshire & North Yorkshire; Merseyside; West Yorkshire	Private sector lead with third sector involvement
Working Links	3	Bristol, Gloucestershire, Somerset & Wiltshire; Dorset, Devon & Cornwall; Wales	Public, private and voluntary company in strategic partnership with Wessex, a Probation Staff mutual
The Reducing Reoffending Partnership	2	Staffordshire & West Midlands; Derbyshire, Leicestershire, Nottinghamshire & Rutland	Equity Joint Venture between private (Ingeus UK) and third sector (St Giles Trust) Crime Reduction Initiatives
MTC Novo	2	Thames Valley; London	Joint Venture between private (MTC and Amey), public (Manchester College) and third sector (RISE – probation staff community interest company; Band of Brothers; Thames Valley Partnership)
EOS Works Ltd	1	Warwickshire & West Mercia	Private sector
Seetec	1	Kent, Surrey & Sussex	Private sector
ARCC	1	Durham Tees Valley	Joint venture between private, public and third sector

Source: Ministry of Justice (2014c).

and Lea, 2014). In this study, the focus is on how practitioners have responded to the proposed changes and how they believed that both probation as an institution and the values of probation staff would be affected by the new structure. Nevertheless, the concerns raised by commentators on what the changes mean for criminal justice and penal policy and theory more widely will also be reflected on and discussed.

Notes

[1] The Parliamentary Select Committee on Public Administration (2002) defined 'public service values' as: social justice; social equity; community responsibility; democratic accountability; impartiality; accountability; trust; equity; probity; and public service.

[2] Napo is the trade union for probation and court staff and represents around 8,000 probation staff (Napo, 2015).

[3] We were unable to contact seven Probation Trusts as contact details were not available or their websites were defunct.

[4] As of 31 March 2014, 16,110 full-time equivalent staff were employed by the Probation Service (Ministry of Justice, 2014a).

[5] The 24-hour strike in November 2013 drew 'thousands' of probation officers and was supported by 80% of those who voted on the strike – the turnout was 46% (BBC, 2013).

[6] For fuller demographic data, see Appendix 2.

2

RESPONDENT VIEWS ON THE PURPOSES AND VALUES OF THE PROBATION SERVICE

Introduction

The brief outline of changes to probation in Chapter One indicated an element of discord between successive governments and probation practitioners in relation to the appropriate purpose and value of the services provided by the Probation Service. In order to provide some context to our interest in probation workers' views of Transforming Rehabilitation (TR), the online survey first asked respondents to explain why they joined the service and subsequently to discuss their views of its purposes and values. We were keen to find out what the value base of our respondents was and how this might affect their perceptions of the proposed changes under TR. The underlying themes emerging from the survey were normative, concerned with probation values, purposes and practices. These were evident in responses to the questions 'Why did you join the Probation Service?' and 'Do you think the Probation Service is underpinned by a particular set of values?'.

Joining the Probation Service

The question on joining the Probation Service was open-ended and 942 respondents answered this question. Answers varied significantly in length, from single-word statements to lengthy explanations. The initial 'cloud' thematic analysis identified the following categories: 21% of respondents identified 'working with people'; 20% identified 'helping people'; 19% identified 'work with offenders'; 11% identified 'protect the public'; 9% identified 'assist people'; and 6% identified 'work in criminal justice'. A number of other categories were identified, including an interest in the job, a desire to work for probation, job security, reducing the number of victims and increasing safety. As respondents were able to give as many reasons as they wished to this open question, any individual could have mentioned any number of the aforementioned answers.

It is clear that the majority of respondents joined the Probation Service for a combination of the most-frequently cited reasons just identified, namely, a desire to 'work with people/offenders' (occasionally 'clients') in a manner generally aligned to offering 'help' and 'assistance'. Indeed, 22 respondents (2%) explicitly mentioned the strapline 'advise, befriend, and assist' to explain their reasons for joining probation. The purpose of this help was the rehabilitation of those being supervised by the service. This was based on a firm belief in the ability of individuals to change and in the Probation Service's ability to facilitate that change. Many other respondents mentioned the reduction of reoffending and it may be that this was regarded by respondents as synonymous with rehabilitation, as has been argued elsewhere (Deering, 2011). Furthermore, it was clear that there was an underlying view that it is the individual's behaviour that is disapproved of and in need of change, rather than the individual being inherently bad, incapable of change and thus in need of punishment. It is also noteworthy that respondents' beliefs about the causes of offending were often explicit within the data and related to individuals who, for a range of reasons, have experienced often multiple disadvantage that has resulted in them making 'bad choices' leading to offending.

In this way, respondents did not subscribe to rational choice theories of crime or to notions of 'bad people doing bad things', but neither were they overly determinist as to the influence of social structure and disadvantage as they recognised a level of individual agency, albeit one influenced by personal history and experience that limits choice and makes offending more likely. Given this context, it seems significant that no mention was made of joining the service with a view to 'punishment' – the word was mentioned in only four responses to this question and then in only general terms, as in having a personal interest in sentencing and punishment and as wanting practice to be not focused solely on this, but to be something more constructive:

I initially joined the Prison Service after graduating [Law] as I have a keen interest in sentencing and punishment. From this experience, I realised that the Probation Service provided a good opportunity for me to work with offenders, both in custody and the community, which would also enable me to have a role in the sentencing process, as well as managing sentences. I was also drawn to the idea of working with a wide number of services and organisations, and have embraced the evolution of this with the introduction of MAPPA [Multi-Agency Public Protection Arrangements], for example, during my career. Since deciding I wanted to work within the criminal justice system I have been a committed public sector employee, and consider myself to not only have a career in this area, but also a vocation.

I had heard about it through a friend and thought it sounded interesting. Then I saw an advert for the training scheme and applied. I wanted to work with people and to try to understand their motivation for offending and to try to find ways of helping people out of destructive patterns of behaviour.

I completed a BSc in Psychology and was interested in crime and behaviour.

I researched job roles in the prison, police and then found probation. I was more interested in the probation approach to the work, ie a higher focus on trying to work with the 'offender' in order to avoid reoffending and not having a sole focus on punishment.

However, in what could be perceived as a sign of risk management becoming an accepted part of probation practice, 11% of responses indicated that respondents had joined the service to protect the public. Several mentions were made of the reduction and management of risk. However, this was generally mentioned not in the context of this being an end of supervision, but, rather, as a means to achieve a reduction in reoffending and the rehabilitation of the individual. In other words, while risk assessment and management formed an important context for supervision, this was not conducted in the narrow sense of management and control as an end in itself (Feeley and Simon, 1992). Alongside this, a minority of respondents mentioned the enforcement of orders. The following illustrate these different reasons for joining the service:

I wanted to be involved in assisting people to change, and where change was not possible, to ensure that the risk they pose was manageable and ensured the safety of the public.

To help men learn to behave differently towards their partners and children.

To write court reports, parole reports and supervise high to medium risk of serious harm offenders. I have a desire to protect the public by making sure offenders comply with court orders and licence conditions. I also enjoy doing some rehabilitation work with them.

While these quotes might be taken as being related to risk assessment and management, what is of interest are the few references to punishment (only four in total). This leads to the tentative conclusion that protecting the public was regarded as best achieved via the reduction of reoffending and the enforcement of orders was related more to accountability to the court, as has been previously identified (Deering, 2011). Of course, in itself, this could be regarded as a form of punishment, in terms of a partial reduction of an individual's liberty (since the Criminal Justice Act 1991), but it seems clear that none of our respondents saw the purpose of supervision as explicitly being related to more limited, punitive ideas of sentencing.

These results replicate other studies in the past decade, and there now seems to be an emerging body of research telling the same story (see, eg, Annison et al, 2008; Deering, 2010; Mawby and Worrall, 2013; Deering et al, 2014). Individuals joined the Probation Service due to a genuine interest in people whose lives have often been characterised by disadvantage and who have made poor choices that have adversely affected victims, the wider community and themselves. Respondents wished to use interpersonal and other skills to help effect change, and, in this way, wished to 'make a difference'. It also seems apparent that the offering of such help was not (and perhaps has never been) based on unconditional assistance; rather, it has been offered with a view to rehabilitation and reduced offending:

I wanted to work for an organisation that helped prevent/reduce crime, thereby reducing victims. I also wanted to work for an organisation which understood how society treats the disadvantaged and assist them to change/try and help them lead more productive and offence-free lifestyles.

I am a people person and believed I could make a difference to people's lives.

Social justice and equality – wanting to make a difference and have a role that I was proud and happy to get out of bed for.

I wanted to help people who were often voiceless and in need of support. I thought it would be a career for life, something I could work up in.

These may be seen to be the underlying reasons for people joining the service throughout its history, despite more recent attempts by the government to change the nature of recruits as part of a concerted effort to move practice away from an approach based upon 'advise, assist and befriend' to one of punishment in the community, risk management and enforcement. There is significant evidence that past efforts to change the nature and composition of probation staff and their occupational culture through recruitment have failed, and it may provide an indication that the nature of the work with offenders may continue to attract individuals motivated by 'people work' regardless of institutional structures and types of employer. Of course, whether individuals can hold on to the values and expectations of work that they enter with is another question.

One interesting way in which our respondents differed from those in the slightly older studies cited earlier is in the mention of desistance. While not mentioned anywhere nearly as often as more proactive ideas of 'helping to change', there was an indication of the influence of recent theories of desistance and the need for probation supervision to assist individual desistance, moving away from a more interventionist, 'treatment' model. The desistance trend is driven partly by academics (eg Farrall, 2002; Weaver and McNeill, 2010), as well as the National Offender Management Service (NOMS) via the 'Offender Engagement Programme' (NOMS, 2013a). In this context, it is worth noting that no mention in this section was made of cognitive-behaviourist approaches or 'what works', despite the level of influence that such approaches appeared to exert over the service's work from the early 1990s. Of course, at this point, respondents were discussing their reasons to join the service, and they may simply not have been aware of these more 'technical' aspects at that time:

> I joined the Probation Service as I wanted to return to working with offenders as a means of protecting future victims and in order to assist individuals in making changes that would significantly impact on theirs and others' lives by stopping offending.

Alongside these main concepts and notions, respondents discussed related areas, such as having an interest in the criminal justice system, in human behaviour in general and specifically in crime. Many had academic qualifications in criminology, sociology and psychology that underlay their interests, but it is also the case that others had simply 'fallen' into the job due to a combination of circumstances and found that it suited them. Many mentioned the enjoyment to be had from the job and the interest it engendered. Another theme was more pragmatic, a minority mentioning only reasons related to stability of employment, levels of annual leave and pension; others mentioned these alongside the other reasons mentioned earlier. On a rather different tack, some respondents mentioned wishing to work for the public sector, occasionally citing 'public sector values' without providing much detail as to what these are, as well as a dislike for 'making money' and practices often associated with the private sector. Of course, such commentary may have been triggered by the immediate context of the ending of probation as a public sector institution:

> I chose a career that I believed would be meaningful and satisfying but would also give me security for the future in terms of long-term and meaningful employment and security in my old age, despite being aware that I could do similar hours and different types of work in the private sector and potentially earn more money.

> Honestly, I had graduated just as the recession hit and found myself without work and on the dole. A case administrator job was advertised and I had always wanted to work within my community doing something that was direct with service users and this seemed to fit.

No data were collected about the age at which respondents joined the service, but it is clear from the responses that, in common with Mawby and Worrall's (2013) study into probation culture, they had either joined relatively soon after completing their education or later after making a switch of career. This latter group mentioned being attracted to the service after varied careers, including the armed forces, police and prison services, as well as a general range of jobs from both the public and private sectors.

Does the Probation Service have an underpinning agreed set of values?

Respondents were also asked: 'Do you think the Probation Service is underpinned by an agreed set of values?'. A total of 937 people responded to this closed question, 68% answering 'yes', 16% answering 'no' and 16% answering 'don't know'. This is itself of interest as while two thirds of respondents answered in the affirmative, one in three felt that the service did not have an agreed set of values underpinning its work or were unsure, and some discussion about why this might have been the case follows. There was some difference between social work-trained staff (CQSW [Certificate of Qualification in Social Work] and DipSW [Diploma in Social Work]) compared to newer DiPS [Diploma in Probation Studies] trained staff, with the former more likely to think that the service did have an agreed set of underpinning values. However, this difference did not reach statistical significance.

There was also a small, but interesting, difference by gender. More women (69%) than men (66%) felt that the Probation Service is underpinned by an agreed set of values ($p < 0.005$). This difference increased once the respondent's status as practitioner or manager was considered. Thus, 67% of female practitioners felt that the Probation Service was underpinned by an agreed set of values compared to 63% of male practitioners ($p < 0.05$); whereas 87% of female managers felt that the Probation Service was underpinned by an agreed set of values compared to 78% of male managers ($p < 0.05$). Probation practice has seen a dramatic and rapid gender shift from being a male-dominated organisation in the 1990s to a female-dominated organisation today (Annison, 2013: 44–45). Annison (2013: 46) reflects on the paradox of the Probation Service undergoing feminisation while governmental rhetoric in relation to probation work, arguably, became more and more punitive and masculine.

It appears that the process of splitting up the Probation Service has led to a further escalation of this gender shift. The latest statistics suggest that, as of September 2014, women now make up 75% of National Probation Service (NPS) staff (Ministry of Justice, 2014a: 5); statistics on the gender balance of Community Rehabilitation Company (CRC) staff were unavailable. Therefore, the small differences in attitudes by gender observed earlier become noteworthy considering the gender balance in the NPS. The feminisation of probation may be interpreted as supporting a return to traditional social work roots. However, Mawby and Worrall (2011: 14) suggested the advent of a 'new breed of female offender manager who is highly organised, computer-literate and focused on public protection'. Our findings reveal that female practitioners and, in particular, female managers seem to be convinced that probation is underpinned by a set of agreed, core values. However, whether these are more 'traditional' or more aligned with Mawby and Worrall's suggestion is unknown at this stage.

The survey question did not specify particular probation values, so an open-ended comments section was provided for those respondents who wished to elaborate on the values referred to in the question. In total, 725 (55% of all respondents; 77% of respondents answering this question) wanted to discuss this further, and an initial analysis showed that the following words and phrases appearing most often: 'people can change' (mentioned in 22% of responses); 'committed to offenders' (20%); 'provide a service' (19%); and 'protect the public' (19%). There were also a number of other responses with below 10% of mentions: 'treating people with respect'; 'being professional'; 'honesty'; operating 'care and control'; and 'social work values'.

The values debate around the Probation Service is a fascinating one, which has more theoretical than empirical contributions. For much of its more recent history, perhaps to the abolition of social work training in the mid-1990s, it was assumed that probation shared the values of 'social work', but these values were themselves seldom defined, except in the requirement within the Probation of Offenders Act 1907 that probation officers 'advise, assist and befriend' their supervisees. This was repealed in the Criminal Justice Act 1991, when the probation order became a sentence of the court and 'punishment in the community', rather than an alternative to a sentence and purely an opportunity to prove an ability to change.

After the 1991 Act, the introduction of National Standards emphasised the management of offenders and sentence enforcement (Home Office, 1992), and the Labour government elected in 1997, although reinstating professional training for probation officers, did not go back to social work training. Instead, it created a new qualification intended to focus more on the protection of the public and the reduction of reoffending (Straw, 1997), and multiple and perhaps contradictory values can be inferred from the aims and objectives given to the service by the Labour government at this time. The 2000 National Standards declared that the service was a 'law enforcement agency' (Home Office, 2000), but the home secretary at the time, David Blunkett, declared that rehabilitation was the 'first priority' (Newburn, 2003: 156). When the National Probation Service for England and Wales was created in 2001, it also revealed a range of aims (Home Office, 2001). There was little discussion of values in the strategy document setting out the creation of the NPS; instead, these have to be inferred from the general content and tone, which emphasised offender management and punishment, although this was to be carried out in a 'humane and equal' manner (Home Office, 2001: 7). Since then, the creation of NOMS and the election of the Coalition government have seen nothing that might lead an observer to reassess government aims for the service and thus its values; these have remained wedded to punishment, public protection and the reduction of reoffending. All of these aims are framed within a remaining commitment to 'rehabilitation' narrowly conceived, as has been shown by the initial Green Paper announcing the 'rehabilitation revolution' (Ministry of Justice, 2010) and by TR itself, although, of course, the methods chosen to achieve rehabilitation in TR are hotly contested.

Policy documents, then, provide a confusing mix of aims and objectives for the Probation Service and not much that could be framed as probation values. Academic commentators have been more prescriptive. Williams (1995) argued that probation values should be based in social work and include the following: an opposition to custody and oppression; a commitment to justice for offenders, while protecting victims; the valuing of offenders as individuals; and a belief in offenders' ability to change facilitated by a purposeful professional relationship. Others argue that the value base should be related to human rights and restorative justice (Nellis, 1999; Nellis and Gelsthorpe, 2003), and Napo has emphasised: respect and trust when working with perpetrators and victims; open and fair treatment for all; the empowerment of individuals in order to reduce the risk of harm to themselves and others; the promotion of equality and anti-discrimination; the promotion of the rights of both perpetrators and victims; and building on individuals' strengths as a vehicle for change (Napo, 2006: 5). This highlights a question of who is best placed to provide a basis for probation values, as summed up by one of our respondents:

> 'Agreed' by whom? The values of the Probation Service are transitory and imposed by government. When the government dogma is to advise, assist and befriend offenders, that is what we are instructed to do. When the government dogma is to protect, rehabilitate and punish, that is what we are instructed to do. Probation values are not underpinned by any moral framework, but are on sale really. I will add that probation officers adhere to their own moral code that leads them to treat offenders with unconditional respect and understanding. Probation officers do try to live to the maxim of 'hate the sin, love the sinner'.

In one empirical study, Robinson and McNeill (2004) reported that practitioners identified public protection, rehabilitation (defined as reducing reoffending) and enforcement as legitimate goals for the service, but that practice needed to be based on a good professional relationship and that this recognised that the basis of much offending is the individual's socio-economic status and their personal experiences. More recently, studies looking at the views of qualified and trainee probation officers (Deering, 2010, 2011) found a considerable level of agreement among the two groups in relation to probation values. There were clear themes about a belief in the ability of individuals to change, as well as the importance of treating all users of the service in a fair, professional and non-discriminatory manner, irrespective of offences committed, echoing Williams (1995) and Napo (2006) cited earlier. In broader terms, there was little to indicate that practitioners emphasised the management of groups based on risk factors or the control of individuals as fundamental values or aims for the service, but, rather, that while risk assessment and risk management were of vital importance, these needed to be individualised, needs-based and flexible, as did the practice of enforcement. Enforcement was influenced by professional judgements about the acceptability of absences, rather than any such absences automatically leading to the breach of an order (see, eg, Deering, 2011: 49–74).

Discussions of probation values are often framed through the lens of criminal justice policy posing threats to the assumed homogeneous values of probation. A special issue of the *European Journal of Probation* (2011, 3[3]) discussed the occupational culture prevalent in probation in England and Wales and provided evidence of a sense of a contested culture defending traditional probation values from organisational and policy pressures. Coping strategies, a degree of covert resistance and alienation were features noted as characterising contemporary probation practice (see, eg, Robinson and Burnett, 2007; Burke and Davies, 2011; Deering, 2011). Mawby and Worrall (2013: 1, emphasis in original) suggest that probation has become an 'area of work where it is necessary for practitioners to act *as if* they believe in the rules about the effectiveness of "risk-crazed governance" while using these rules in a way that achieves meaning'.

For most of our research respondents, it appears that the service has continued to operate with multiple values, but these are underpinned by a fundamentally humanistic approach that values each person as an individual human being of intrinsic worth. This view does not ignore the harm that any individual may have caused, but sees this as behaviour to be addressed and that can be changed. It is thus the act that is disapproved of, not the person:

[Probation values are a] belief in the essential worth of all people, that all are capable of change for the better.

A belief in the worth and value of every human.

Unconditional positive regard.

That our work within rehabilitation is underpinned by the belief that personal change is possible, that resistance to that change is normal and that we don't jettison people because of it. That a caring society seeks to help the disadvantaged and those in need or those that have not had the basic support when young. That we do this because it is a moral social principle. It is not about assessing people on a spread sheet and looking for a profit margin.

Acknowledgement that people are not born evil. Belief in an individual's capacity to change.

One thing I think most good staff members share is a fundamental kind of respect for people – a belief in a common humanity and capacity for change and growth. It's hard to put into words but it goes for service users, victims, everyone in society, rather than seeing our clients as somehow strange and separate and 'other'. It's a humanising, integrative and supportive view of people – and sometimes that means telling them and others hard truths and taking restrictive action, which can and should be supportive just as much as the rest of our work.

The values that I and my colleagues share are about the individual and seeing a person not just an offence. That they are a father, son, brother, and can play an important and valued role in society.

This strongly resonates with the most frequently mentioned value (22% of respondents), which was a belief in the ability of an individual to change. However, it rarely appeared alone, usually being combined with a number of other values around treating people with respect, being non-judgemental and anti-discriminatory, and having a strong sense that offending has its roots in multiple disadvantage and social injustice, rather than rational choice, while also accepting the role of agency and the damage caused by offending:

> Without an agreed set of values, how would we consistently model desired attitudes and behaviour? Off the top of my head, these values include: that everyone has the potential to change for the better; that treating people with respect and modelling how you would like them to treat others is more effective than being judgemental; anti-discrimination.

> That all humans are born equal and a blank sheet and life makes an impact which is sometimes negative but can be turned around … probation treats people fairly and offers them a chance to change.

> Being positive about individuals and communities, and their abilities to change; being non-judgemental about our clients but actively challenging their actions when necessary; zero tolerance towards discrimination and oppression.

> Treating people fairly, openly and with respect. Valuing diversity. A belief in the capacity of people to change. An uncompromising stance against the harm caused by crime.

> Equal and fair treatment of all from the time they are first in court to the end of any sentence that they might get. Non-judgemental and supportive treatment from all staff. Focus on preventing future victims. Honesty, integrity, fair and impartial treatment. No one is considered beyond rehabilitation and a second chance. Everyone is capable of change.

> Acceptance that we all make mistakes and that all are entitled to overcome their mistake. Non-judgemental but challenging view of

offending. Belief that social justice for offenders and victims should underpin a decent society.

These views may be regarded as examples of 'traditional' probation values. Alongside these, it is evident that they have been joined by others, possibly as a result of a direct drive by government towards the risk and enforcement agendas. Other research mentioned earlier indicates that while many practitioners have accepted the risk and enforcement agenda in principle and support their importance, they do so with perhaps a different emphasis from government. In this way, risk assessment is important not simply to manage potential harm, but to identify how best to work with an individual to effect change, as well as the occasional need to take more direct measures to protect the public:

> That the law must be upheld. That offenders should and must be given an opportunity to adjust their behaviour. That we accept, as a society, people offend for many different reasons and that we need to understand this in order to address it. That victims need to be protected.

> To be concerned about the outcomes for the offender and the community. To bring about a just and fair delivery of justice. To be non-judgemental, yet critical, of offenders' behaviour. To value the person not the offence. To have the public and victims as our primary consideration.

> I think the Probation Service is underpinned by a core value of robust public protection. It also encompasses values of the individual, both for staff and offenders, in that each working relationship is unique and tailored towards achieving objectives for that individual. It also has strong values for belief in rehabilitation and that people can become offence-free and lead fulfilling lives within the community.

I joined the service when there was an emphasis on public protection above all other things. I agree that this should be our main focus but you cannot do this without working with the individual and understanding their difficulties and circumstances. I feel probation work has always been about managing risk, as well as advising, assisting and befriending. My colleagues with 20 years' plus experience have always done this but feel their work was with a marginalised group of people, I think they were of the view that you cannot lessen those risks without supporting the person and trying to improve their lot.

To undertake what is required to engage and work with people who have committed offences to encourage them to rehabilitate and reintegrate into mainstream society. To supervise and monitor their progress and when necessary to enforce progress or initiate other measures to be engaged.

Are probation values under pressure?

Generally, comments about values were consistent with, and thus reaffirmed, many of the values associated with probation in the literature mentioned earlier. However, others argued that over the last (roughly) 20 years, probation values have come under pressure from the government promoting its new agendas of punishment, public protection, risk and enforcement. Moreover, this 'decline' in values (as it is seen by many respondents) has accelerated more recently and reached a peak with TR. There was, therefore, something of a sub-narrative of change and decline and of individuals having to 'hang onto' and defend their own values in the face of a changing government agenda.

Alongside this was the minority feeling that values were becoming more contested than they had been in the past and that some respondents considered their colleagues to hold views of which they did not approve:

[Values are agreed] only in part – most staff appear to regard their vocation as social work-based rather than public protection-based.

Napo has quite recently tried to review and reassert 'professional standards' (a piece of work I am very proud to have contributed to) but I do not believe there is any consensus about values amongst the workforce anymore and am still capable of being shocked by how hard-nosed, uncompromising and 'right-wing' some colleagues can be in their attitudes to our clients.

Over time and with a move towards 'enforcement', new staff have come into the service with very different values and expectations – they are not mine.

I think there is tension between enforcement and rehabilitation, mainly because the term 'enforcement' is applied too literally by some practitioners/managers.

Over the last 20 years, people have been attracted to the job for a much wider range of reasons and the changes in training have led to a variety of different priorities – some do ascribe to what I outline above, others are much more punitive in approach and some seem to dislike offenders altogether.

However, research studies looking at shifts in attitudes and evidence from our survey do not support this suggestion (Deering, 2010, 2011). It appears that attempts to recruit a new breed of probation staff have failed to a significant extent. Nevertheless, some respondents expressed strong views about the attempts of various governments to undermine probation values, which had been supported, partly, by senior probation management:

I think the Probation Service might once have been underpinned by social work values, which valued individuals and believed in their capacity for change. Since 2000 or thereabouts, it has 'consciously uncoupled' from social work and tried to redefine itself as a criminal justice agency. It has taken a tougher, more punitive stance.

Yes and no. I think the front-line staff relate to supporting the offender, protecting the public and reducing reoffending, but I feel that this has been lost by senior management and those governing probation. The drive seems less about doing the job and more about targets, ticking boxes and data recording.

I think the individuals bring their values; however, Trusts' leadership appear to be fighting for their own agendas.

I think that the Probation Service used to be underpinned by a set of values that had integrity and strength. However, I also believe that, today, these values have been systematically eroded by successive governments with their own political agendas. Gone is the belief and determination to help offenders to address their criminogenic needs – whatever these may be. Gone is much of the funding that was used to achieve this. Gone is the transparency and openness of our approach, replaced with a closed shop and secretive approach by the MoJ [Ministry of Justice], senior managers and the Trust board. Gone is the importance of actually helping, assisting and befriending – and in has come 'managing offenders', with ticking the right boxes and completing the case records and assessments more important than actual working with offenders.

As time has gone on, and especially during 'moral panics' and government media-driven agendas, I would suggest that senior management within the Probation Service and NOMS, in particular, have shown a lack of respect for those we work with, and in an effort to be seen to 'punish' and 'protect the public', seem to make efforts to ignore the rights of those high-risk offenders we manage and ignore that rehabilitation can take place.

The marketisation of probation added another dimension to the question of values. While probation staff may be willing to accept different emphases on risk management and public protection, they are finding the introduction of market principles into probation difficult to reconcile with traditional probation values. This leaves practitioners increasingly at odds with government, something that is likely to accelerate in the commercial world of the CRC:

> More and more, I consider [myself] 'at odds' with the Probation Service values. We label the people we work with and create more obstacles for the most vulnerable members of the community. The current emphasis appears to be control, monitor, assess/judge. I think there is less understanding of how people develop and what is required to integrate those on the edges of society.

> These seem to have slipped towards expediency and market forces. How can what we do be driven by profit?

> Probation values have been lost in the emphasis on targets, management and money. WE SHOULD NOT BE A MONEY-MAKING VENTURE!!!! (Sorry for shouting.)

> Evidencing social inclusion is so important in probation practice. The integrity of the service is measured by how we work with such a diverse client group. Compare a typical Trust with, for example, Sodexo or Capita? If any of those organisations were able to engage with a service user with a credible social inclusion agenda, it would be the Trust. We know that in terms of desistance, it's the relationship with the probation officer that eventually facilitates real change. How can organisations like A4E or Sodexo have the kind of 'values in practice' (not on a bid webpage) that service users can identify with and, more importantly, work with?

This perceived change and decline is seen as taking place as the result of government interference due to the increasing politicisation of criminal justice in general, including probation, fitting in with general theories of the new penality and the culture of control (Feeley and Simon, 1992; Garland, 2001). As mentioned, other studies have identified nuances in probation values as reported by practitioners, but the pattern of these responses seems to indicate a level of division between respondents and increasing disillusion with the 'state of probation'.

A dividing service – management and practitioners at odds?

When management were mentioned in the open comment sections (and not forgetting that 15% of respondents overall were management grades), they were largely regarded: as complicit in the changes to probation; as becoming removed from front-line practice; as submitting to managerialist tendencies; and even oppressive and bullying behaviour towards practitioners in their pursuit of targets and outputs. Managers were regarded as less interested in the quality of supervision and outcomes. Differences in the attitudes of probation practice and values between practitioner and management grades were obvious in a number of the closed questions. There were significant differences between probation officers, of whom two thirds (66%) agreed that the Probation Service was underpinned by an agreed set of values, compared with 82% of managers,[1] and 63% of other probation staff ($p <$ 0.000), revealing perhaps more disillusion, as well as direct experience of the tension between proclaimed institutional and individual values among probation officer grades. This echoes findings elsewhere (Deering, 2011; Mawby and Worrall, 2011: 16; Robinson et al, 2014) that also saw practitioners beginning to identify management as 'other' to some degree and increasingly divorced from practice.

Additionally, practitioners, that is, probation officers and Probation Service officers (61%), were less likely to think that offender supervision needed to be more 'flexible and creative' than managers (75%) or other probation staff (65%) ($p <$ 0.05). Similarly, there were differences between the three groups in the extent to which they supported government policy on extending supervision to those released from short-term prison sentences: 73% of practitioners supported this policy; 85% of managers; and 82% of other probation staff ($p < 0.05$).

The differences in views around the question of an agreed set of values in the Probation Service emerged most strongly among those who felt that their job had not lived up to their expectations. Respondents felt let down by management and accused them of a lack of knowledge, poor leadership and putting their personal careers before the needs of probation staff and offenders:

> Constant political interference by those with personal ambition attempting to grandstand and promote their own careers by imposing change top-down within the criminal justice system, for change's sake alone, without a reliable 'evidence base' or allowance of evaluation of the last initiative before the next change is made. Failure of leadership within the Probation Service itself to rebuff such political misadventure, prioritising instead their own career ambitions, as willing administrators of anything. Institutional culture of 'managerialism', ie, blind adherence to achievement of process targets rather than outcomes. Priority to league tables and organisational plaudits. Equivalent stupidity to NHS [National Health Service] acceptance of ambulances queuing around the block, provided a target appears to be met. People who have committed offences receiving second-rate support and oversight, in direct consequence of all the above. I came from the commercial sector. Even after 10+ years in the Probation Service, I have not ceased to be shocked by the complacency of our leadership. We are a service organisation which accepts failure as the predicted and actual outcome for the majority of our service users. Something is clearly very wrong.

> Much more target-driven – targets often seem to bear little relationship to what we are trying to achieve as a service. Less support from senior staff and more blame culture than I thought. Absence of knowledge base/experience from senior staff was a surprise.

Poor senior managers who insisted upon workloads that were far too onerous for me to devote time to managing risk and rehabilitation. Poor management in general. A blame culture that discouraged officers from taking risks and learning from experience. Dreadful Information Technology that hinders rather than supports officers in their day-to-day tasks. Poor staff management. Abysmal care for officers' well-being, resulting in high stress levels and sick absences. Culture of bullying that remained unaddressed for years despite people making complaints.

The values of senior management are not the values of practitioners.

I think it used to be but gone are the days of advise, assist and befriend. I think colleagues and management are working to different values. My main aim is to keep my head above water and to make sure I look after my own health and stress levels. It is difficult to focus fully on much else.

No longer [are there a set of agreed values] ... [the] emphasis in management appears to be 'I'm alright Jack'.

The emerging divisions and, in some cases, outright hostility between management and practitioners is not a preserve of the Probation Service. Similar trends have been noted in the police and the Prison Service (in relation to prisons, see Liebling, 2004; in relation to the police, see Brown et al, 1996; Feilzer and Trew, 2012). Crewe and Liebling (2012a: 180) discuss a variety of management styles and manager 'ideal types' in the prison system, with a majority categorised as managerialists, who prioritise 'smooth management and efficiency'. The divisions between practitioners and managers may form part of the effects of changes in the administration of criminal justice organisations through the introduction of managerialism, which resulted in a more bureaucratic approach and the distancing of management from practice, particularly at middle-manager level. These structures are designed to limit the ability of individuals to understand the organisation's overall strategy and goals, and with that, practitioners' agency is threatened and decision-making is homogenised (Cheliotis, 2006: 318–319). Managers within these structures are accountable for the delivery of performance targets and, as a consequence, may be seen as the symbol and tool of the threats to discretion and decision-making powers of individual front-line practitioners. Thus, broader resistance among practitioners against the pressures of penal managerialism finds expression in distancing processes between managers and front-line staff.

Having considered our respondents' views on the purposes and values of the service, Chapter Three looks at whether the current and likely future state of governance will bring an end to what we have called the ideal of probation as a public sector endeavour.

Note

[1]   In our analysis, we distinguished between management and other probation staff but we did not separate out senior management as grades above team manager only made up 26 of our respondents.

3

IS THIS THE END OF AN IDEAL?

This chapter looks at views about the extent to which working for the Probation Service had lived up to expectations, and had this not been the case, why might this be. This is then considered in the wider context of considering whether the ideal of the service is in the process of being actively unravelled by the government in a way that the values expressed in previous chapters will be unable to transcend.

Has the service lived up to expectations?

Not surprisingly perhaps, in the context of the (minority) view of a decline in values discussed in previous chapters, there was a clearly identifiable theme of the service only partly living up to respondents' expectations. Of course, this may be the 'norm' among most occupational groups and it is probably unlikely that a similar question asked of other groups would differ in this regard. In particular, professional groups in the criminal justice system are in the midst of experiencing the effects of budget cuts across the public sector, as well as a significant amount of institutional change. A recent survey of prison officers, for example, found that 70% of prison officers regretted their choice of job and 50% were seriously considering leaving their job in the near future. The report on prison officer stress and work-related well-being noted that the profession suffered from higher levels of 'psychological distress than other occupational groups including "emotionally demanding" professions such as the police and social work' (Kinman et al, 2014: 3).

Our probation respondents were asked: 'Has working for the service lived up to your expectations?'. Of those who responded (n = 959), some 38% said that the service had done so, but a small overall majority, 51%, said that it only partly had, leaving 11% feeling that it had not. Given that the category 'partly lived up to expectations' was an option, those choosing either of the other two presumably felt strongly that the service had/had not fulfilled their expectations. Similarly, given the significant changes to which the service has been subject in recent decades, it is not surprising that the largest number of respondents felt that it had only partly lived up to expectations. However, this is in contrast to earlier findings by Annison et al (2008: 264) among recently qualified probation officers, where the majority of respondents stated that their expectations were being met.

Perhaps this partial satisfaction reflects the fact that despite the many structural and policy changes affecting probation, the essential core of the work, that is, engaging with individuals in an attempt to facilitate or encourage change, while possibly under pressure, had not altered substantively, at least in the eyes of practitioners. This situation is reflected in a number of other studies (Farrow, 2004; Napo, 2007; Robinson and Burnett, 2007; Mawby and Worrall, 2013), which identify the enduring commitment of practitioners to this core purpose despite varying views about changes to governance and official policy foisted upon them by government and senior management. Indeed, as long ago as 2004, following significant restructuring and the creation of the National Probation Service for England and Wales in 2001, Farrow (2004) reported on a study in two probation areas with probation officers of at least 10 years' experience. Farrow's participants had worked through the period that had seen the creation under the Criminal Justice Act 1991 of the probation order as a sentence of the court, the coming of 'community punishment' and National Standards. They had also seen the emergence of the risk and public protection agendas and, to accompany all these developments, the emergence of managerialism, auditing and accounting mechanisms.

Farrow's respondents fitted clearly into the pattern seen in other studies of why people have joined the service over the decades mentioned earlier, and, of interest, she reported that their commitment to this core purpose – to 'probation work' and 'its clients' – had survived these changes. However, their commitment to the organisation had not been as robust and had resulted in general alienation (Farrow, 2004: 210). The main reasons for this were: the increased bureaucratisation of the service; the culture of audit and control and the subsequent loss of autonomy; the overall workload increase on administrative and not professional tasks; and the notion that management was becoming divorced from practice.

Robinson and Burnett (2007) interviewed probation officers about their perception of the implications of the emergence of the National Offender Management Service (NOMS) and the introduction of a system of offender management. They found a general uncertainty about the implications among the probation officers interviewed and a degree of ambivalence (Robinson and Burnett, 2007: 324). Particular concerns were expressed about the notion of contestability and a general erosion of direct one-to-one work with offenders (Robinson and Burnett, 2007: 329–30). Mawby and Worrall (2013: 109–110) looked at reasons for joining the service and reactions to perceived dissatisfaction in the workplace, noting that few probation practitioners actually left, most finding ways in which to manage their work to their own satisfaction via 'bending' but not breaking the rules and generally finding ways in which to get job satisfaction from the core purpose despite (and certainly not because of) top-down changes.

When looking at our respondents who did comment on this question ($n = 817$; some 85% of those who answered the main, closed question), it is again of interest that their reasons for joining and their attitudes to the service, where these reveal some dissatisfaction, echoed those interviewed by Farrow (2004) and Mawby and Worrall (2013). Moreover, although responding to questions a decade later than Farrow's (2004) respondents, their concerns about the direction of the service had very strong parallels and went back further than specific issues around 'Transforming Rehabilitation' (TR). Although the percentage of those indicating that the service had partly lived up to their expectations represented a narrow overall majority, from those who commented, it is also evident that they wanted to express the ways in which the service had not lived up to their expectations, rather than the ways in which it had. There were positive comments, but these were in the minority and tended to concentrate on the work of colleagues and the inherent purpose of the job, rather than any connection to NOMS or government policy. However, the following positive comments are examples of ways in which the service had lived up to expectations by providing a good working environment, job satisfaction through the perception of achieving positive change in others and good work life–balance:

> Great organisation with fantastic colleagues who do excellent work.

> Sometimes, there have been real changes for people which is nice to see/witness; work with sex offenders in particular has been intellectually fascinating; staff/colleagues have mostly been good to work with too.

> In the main, I have enjoyed my job and think that I have motivated people to make positive changes in their lives.

> I thought it would be interesting and it has [been], definitely challenging and I think we've helped some of those we've supervised and protected/prevented further victims.

> I have been able over the years to engage effectively with offenders and make some difference to some people even if only small steps. I'd like to think that many of the people who I have worked with have benefitted from my skills, experience and background.

> I have been very humbled by being allowed to undertake this work and it has mainly been a pleasure to work for the service.

I love my job. It is varied and interesting and never boring and it is worthwhile. What else could I be doing that would have a better impact on our society?

Working for the service has gone far beyond my expectations. I'm astonished to think that it's now probably over 12 years since I first applied, and the range of people that I've met, and the things that I've done during this time has been astonishing.

To date, I have found the service comprised of staff who are dedicated and motivated and, despite budget cuts and a target-driven culture, undertaking innovative and creative work to protect the public and assist in offender rehabilitation.

Good colleagues, good training and development. Good Trust, which valued staff and offered interesting career opportunities. Interesting and professionally satisfying role.

Very good employer for recognising work–life balance.

However, as mentioned, most of the open responses illustrated how the service had not lived up to expectations, rather than how it had:

I still enjoy working face-to-face with offenders. I do not like the bureaucracy that now governs what we do.

Over time, the number of working hours and workload has increased significantly with the result that taking TOIL [time off in lieu] or leave can be problematical. Our annual leave entitlement has been cut and our pay frozen.

Under-resourced and overworked, any number of people off with work-related stress – people struggling to keep heads about workload – this month's crisis workload is next month's baseline

– difficult to remain professional or objective – feel completely devalued.

For the first seven years of my service, probation worked very well. Once the idea of privatisation started creeping in, things started to go downhill, rapidly. We now have a hierarchy whereby our chief and many of the senior managers have absolutely no idea what is happening on the 'shop floor'.

When I came in to probation in 1999, there was the chance to work in a therapeutic way to bring about change – particularly in programmes. However, this has slowly gone out of the window and has been replaced with a factory-like set-up with inputs and outputs rather than seeing offenders as people who need help.

I loved my job for several years (coming up to 25) and I still believe in the work we do. In the last decade, I think it has become overcomplicated and over-managed. I think this has been government-led and this has resulted in too many projects, flow charts, codes and improvement projects.

Some statistically significant differences were expressed between our respondent groups in answer to the attitudinal statements linked to this issue. Those who felt that working for the Probation Service had not lived up to expectations (35%) were significantly less likely to think that probation was underpinned by a set of agreed values than those who felt it had, either partly (62%) or completely (85%) ($p < 0.000$). This was one of the few areas where respondents differed from each other, but it does seem to indicate a clear division of opinion influenced by personal experiences and their impact on wider perceptions of shared values.

A number of respondents had clearly become very disillusioned by the service and its practices. Importantly, this was related to the way in which probation had changed, rather than any dissatisfaction or disagreement with the core purpose or what it should be. The following responses are typical:

> I have become increasingly disillusioned with the leadership nationally, and within teams, and the lack of any real support structure for staff working with increasingly difficult and high-risk cases within an organisational structure which has been more obsessed with meeting targets on OASys [Offender Assessment System] completion than on what actually happens face-to-face with service users.

> My early career was very different, I felt listened to and had supportive managers, good team working, there was more creativity and variety in the work we did, engaging with local communities more for example. In terms of career development, I feel let down by probation as a career in over 20 years of work as a highly skilled and well-regarded practitioner who has achieved independent recognition of my abilities.

> There isn't enough room in the box [to answer this question]! Basically the service has turned its back on decades of social work to follow an Americanised path of 'management' of 'offenders' @ the expense of building a personal relationship of trust with clients. It would take me two hours to answer this question properly.

While some of the disappointment with the service was linked to recent and forthcoming changes, there were other factors that influenced respondents' views on probation. These comments were minority views, but, nevertheless, they serve as an important reminder that it is easy to fall into a trap of nostalgia when discussing the demise of probation as a public institution. Perhaps assumptions of a golden age of, or general consensus on, rehabilitation and probation are to be expected and quite natural. However, Zedner (2002: 344) discusses the fallacy of assuming a consensus on rehabilitation and probation even in the 'good old days' of penal welfarism of the 1960s as such debates existed at that time (see, eg, Bottoms and McWilliams, 1979; Raynor, 2012). Zedner's account points to concerns over a lack of a normative framework in relation to fairness and justice, doubts over efficacy, and excessive intrusion into individual offenders' lives, as well as the limited use of probation orders in practice. In this context, some of the views questioning the Probation Service's recent credentials as a liberal, progressive and humanistic organisation are highlighted here:

> The most reactive organisation that it is possible to imagine. Overly bureaucratic and without any scope for creativity or individuality. Overly politically correct. Constantly changing for the worse. Rife with nepotism and cronyism.

> High caseloads, bureaucracy, target-driven performance pay to managers, ideologically driven/unilateral political intervention in provision, public sector demonisation, treatment with barely disguised contempt, use of crime as a political expedient/distraction, juvenile propaganda, impoverishment of public funding with consequences for offending, privatisation as an end with attendant corruption, all and much more leading to demoralisation, illness, redundancy/resignation.

> I have found the Probation Service antiquated in some of its philosophy and theory. I was surprised to see much of the more progressive thinking that had become everyday practice in social work had not even been heard of, or considered as yet, in probation. Many of the newer officers are ingrained with the dogma of CBT [cognitive behavioural therapy] and are unable to see the bigger picture. I was thankful when I trained in BBR [Building Better Relationships] [which replaced the old domestic violence programme, IDAP (Integrated Domestic Abuse Programme)]. The trainer was one of the programme writers, a forensic psychologist, and we discussed the fact that impulsive thinking actually exists – this was completely alien to the more recently trained probation officers [POs] who were convinced that 'thoughtful behaviours'

dominated all actions. Many POs suffer with rigid thinking and the Probation Service as a whole has certainly left behind empathy and diversity, selecting instead to head down the enforcement path without considering other routes for treatment.

Only a small number of respondents mentioned wishing to leave the service as a result of their level of disaffection. As with Mawby and Worrall's (2013) findings, this level of disillusion did seem very much a minority view, although, of course, it is unknown whether others felt similarly but were constrained, perhaps mindful of the difficulties inherent in changing occupations due, at the very least, to financial and other commitments. Interestingly, this seems to have been contradicted somewhat by responses later in the survey to attitudinal statements, where in response to the question 'I am considering looking for another job because of my concerns about my own future and the future of the Probation Service', 76% agreed, 9% disagreed and 15% neither agreed nor disagreed. This may be due to a reaction to a 'sound bite' attitudinal statement that refers to 'considering looking' for another job, whereas the responses to the comments section were unprompted:

I wish I had chosen another career, and now I fear it is too late to change.

The past two years have been unbearable in terms of how Trusts seem to change to being overly dictatorial, making inexplicable decisions – this then being followed by something even more inexplicable, ie, TR. If I could afford it, I would go now.

It is clear that for a small group of respondents, working for the Probation Service did not live up to their expectations to any great degree. For many more, it only partly did. In some cases, this related to unhappiness with the organisational structures and individual situations. In many instances, however, dissatisfaction related to a mismatch between the values of the individuals joining the service and their perception of changing probation values.

If 'values' are 'in decline', why might this be?

The preceding discussion of 'job satisfaction' presented a strong theme of at least partial disillusion with the values, policies and practices of the service as it has developed over the past decade or so as a result of government-led change. While some aspects, such as the management of risk and enforcement, were seen as reasonable and to be welcomed, in the main, successive governments were seen as making the wrong changes to the service for the wrong reasons. In brief, recent changes were seen as driven by ideology, underpinned by an intolerance of offenders and offending and the promotion of 'punishment' rather than assistance. Qualitative responses making these points were backed up by responses to attitudinal statements. In response to the statement 'The government's ideas for change contained within Transforming Rehabilitation are not based on any evidence of the greater effectiveness of the private or third sectors in working with offenders', 96% of respondents agreed. Similarly, 82% of respondents agreed that 'The government is pursuing these changes as a result of an ideological commitment to reducing the size of the state'.[1]

These views were overlaid by other concerns about the emergence of bureaucracy, managerialism and the culture of audit, and the removal of management from practice in order to oversee the achievement of government-imposed targets. In some cases, this had been made worse by what was regarded by some as a bullying approach by some managers and a blame culture and lack of support for staff in practitioner grades. This was further exacerbated by the resultant emphasis on record-keeping, which had resulted in a considerable drop in face-to-face work (Napo, 2010), made worse by what were seen as inefficient information technology (IT) systems. These themes pre-date TR, but the National Probation Service (NPS)–Community Rehabilitation Company (CRC) split seems to have brought existing IT deficiencies to a head (Leftly, 2014c). It is noteworthy that not a single response welcomed these developments, with the following comments being typical:

> I believe some of the work we undertake has been thwarted by ever-changing government policies, which, in many cases, have not contributed to the reduction of reoffending. Notably, the bureaucratic obsession with form-filling and also repeating that information on a myriad of forms all containing similar information. The current government TR agenda is chaotic, untested and poorly thought out.

> Change of direction in that it became an enforcement agency with restrictive National Standards that did not allow for the complex and sometimes chaotic lifestyles of those we work with (staff and clients). The training now trained enforcers not thinkers and was at risk of attracting folk who didn't naturally adhere to the fundamental values of probation. The loss of the use of the word 'probation' was also disappointing – probation order changed to community order and we were directed to use the title offender manager rather than probation officer.

> It was great from 1979 to the end of the 90s. Thereafter, it went downhill as the profession became more geared to unnecessary bureaucracy and less to the needs of people.

> I think the service took a turn for the worse when it got obsessed with law enforcement and forgot that it was there to help disadvantaged people and viewed them as being totally responsible for their circumstances without compassion.

> My first year, post-qualification in 1992, was encouraging and I began to believe I had chosen wisely in terms of my values and commitment. Within the course of about 18 months, however, everything began to change, beginning with the introduction of National Standards. From that point on, the slow destruction of the

Probation Service as an ethical public institution of integrity and professional quality has been accomplished seamlessly, regardless of the party-political persuasion of the administration, through non-stop political interference, and the ever-burgeoning subcultures of bureaucracy, managerialism and the hegemony of IT. The driving forces have been nakedly harnessed to the retention of political power by pandering to a tabloid mentality with regard to crime and the clients of our service, and a relentless dumbing-down of the public debate about justice and the law.... This effectively moved the emphasis away from any structural critique of society, from a focus on inequality, employment, welfare, housing and mental health issues, to an overarching and, in time, unexamined assumption that 'offenders' get into trouble because they don't think like the rest of us and need to be 'pro-socially' remodelled into being more compliant and 'acceptable' units. These predominant ideologies are anathema to my own beliefs and, over many years, have consigned me to an unending and largely futile rearguard action in an attempt to remain true to my convictions and to the now barely perceptible traces of a once-proud service to whose values I had been prepared to commit my working life.... Romantically, I have for some time cast myself as a resistance fighter in a beloved, but thoroughly occupied, country. In some ways, this expresses my response to the obvious question: 'If you are so unhappy, why don't you just leave?'. This is my home; why should I go? Where should I go? I am not the one who has destroyed it in the name of ignorant populism and easy votes.

Essentially, the 'profession' was destroyed and insidiously reduced to almost childlike properties, ticking senseless boxes and being subjected to differing subjective orders. There appears little, or much less, interest in the 'client' now and an emphasis on completing targets, many of which have no apparent sense or purpose.

Since I joined in 2002, there have been changes to the service, it seems every couple of years, brought about by the politicians, restricting and reducing funding over the years. It seems the Probation Service is now the butt of blame to these politicians and their cronies within NOMS, which itself has been a gigantic waste of public funds.

These changes have been unfolding over as long as 20 years, but it is clear that the coming of TR has taken the situation to a new level for respondents by completely undermining the bedrock of the basis and purpose of their work in probation. TR was seen as ideologically driven and unwelcome from a range of perspectives: in principle (as many oppose privatisation and the making of profit from punishment); as deskilling for those being placed in a CRC; as undermining of security in terms of employment; and as removing the possibility of progression from Probation Service officer to probation officer by not requiring the CRCs to implement the Probation Qualifications Framework (PQF):

> Absolutely has [lived up to expectations] – until now, when I will cease to be a public servant. This makes a huge difference to me.

> Until very recently, I have felt that assisting with public safety and helping people make positive changes to their lives was at the heart of what we do. Unfortunately, this current government and its obsession with privatising public services has really deviated us from our true objectives.

> Loved my job from 1993 until about 2004, but things have changed for the worse. No longer centred on offenders, but on targets. The TR agenda has now worsened things even more with experienced, highly skilled officers being forced into the CRCs having written PSRs [Pre-Sentence Reports] and worked with high risk of harm offenders for years – neither of which they will be able to do again, so are looking to retrain.

> I have been demoted to CRC – no longer allowed to work with high-risk offenders – the reason I undertook two years' hard training. I have been isolated from other PO colleagues on my team who have all been assigned to NPS. I am no longer able to do the role I trained for.

This last comment points to a wider concern over the professional status of those probation officers who have been allocated to the CRCs. The process of allocation has been questioned by Napo and other probation representatives and there have been suggestions that staff were allocated randomly by 'drawing employee numbers out of a hat', a claim rigorously rejected by the Ministry of Justice (Politics.co.uk, 2014). In limiting NPS and CRC staff exposure to a range of offenders with varying levels of risk, the split also raises concerns over deskilling staff and the impact of working exclusively with high-risk and serious offenders. The lack of career opportunities as a result of TR was mentioned repeatedly in the following comments, and 65% of respondents disagreed with the Likert statement that 'Working for the private sector will open up more career opportunities for me'. In fact, there are considerable concerns over the security of employment in the CRCs beyond the seven months' guaranteed protection by the National Agreement (NNC, 2014: D3/2–5):

> I joined the service some 15 years ago and in between then and the inexorable drift to the TR programme, the work was always hard, but there was a large element of job satisfaction. I now feel stripped of my professional qualifications and experience and have become a functionary, locked into my computer, indeed, almost as an administrator, with minimal time to see offenders.

> It has been a great service with a few ups and downs until TR came along.

> Until TR it [the service] had lived up to expectations.

I have job satisfaction. But I am concerned about job security in the light of what is going on and I have been getting headaches and feeling stressed.

Appreciated the training and support but disappointed that I will not be able to do the PQF to become a PO.

It did [live up to expectations] until the TR came in. Now I feel undervalued, deskilled and vulnerable. Chances for career progression vanished.

I am disappointed in the Trust that my career development has been halted because of the lack of opportunity to progress. Up until the TR came about, I was quite happy in the knowledge I had a lifelong career – I never considered doing anything else – now I am seeking alternative employment, which is heart-breaking.

Clearly, the service has lived up to some people's expectations and has, in part, to an overall majority. However, it is the case that the majority of comments expressed sadness, anger and frustration at the direction imposed upon the service by government, which has now reached its height with the ending of the service as a unified public body:

I have loved working with offenders; I have never been bored except when completing OASys. However, over the last few years, I have felt totally disillusioned by the prescriptive nature of the work, the fact that I spend most of my time inputting data and working long hours just to meet meaningless targets. I have felt bullied and undervalued.

What should be the job of the Probation Service?

We complete this chapter by considering what respondents thought the Probation Service should be doing. This was asked without reference to the forthcoming split in the service, so it forms part of the overall view of the probation ideal. Some 897 respondents (68% of the overall sample) commented and the initial thematic analysis provided a number of areas to consider. While the biggest single category was 'manage risk' (mentioned by 23%), a number of other categories could be combined into a broad category of supervision, which included mention of: rehabilitation; addressing offending; managing sentences; working with offenders; assisting offenders; and reducing offending. These categories together totalled some 95% of responses.[2]

While there were clearly overlaps with earlier questions, this question explored a further normative dimension: that of respondents' 'wish lists' for the aims and purposes of the service. With regards to the aims of 'probation work' after the break-up of the service and the creation of the NPS and CRCs, TR only discussed this in very general ways (Ministry of Justice, 2013), concentrating on the punishment of offenders, protecting the public and reducing reoffending. The main thrust of the TR document was around the reorganisation of supervision and the break-up of the service, of governance rather than underpinning principles. However, our respondents had a clear idea of what the service or any successor organisations should be doing. As mentioned, although managing risk received the biggest single 'mention count', when considering contributions in the round, it was engagement with individuals with a view to behavioural change that was clearly the most important purpose. What was also clear is that words and phrases such as 'rehabilitation', 'reducing reoffending', 'working with people' and so on were largely used synonymously. Moreover, public protection was generally seen as best achieved via rehabilitation and the reduction in reoffending, although the need to manage those relatively few individuals who pose a higher risk of harm was stressed. Few respondents mentioned a single purpose, with most emphasising the need to engage people and, thus, protect the public:

> To help people recognise that they have the skills to change because
> a lot of people don't think they can. To protect the public from the
> risk of emotional, physical, financial and sexual harm.

To enable service users to reduce their reoffending by making the positive changes which might allow them to desist from future offending. To protect the public through robust, dynamic and continuous risk assessment.

To ensure offenders face up to the harm (whether physical, practical, emotional, etc) they cause to others, to support them in making changes to reduce their risk of reoffending and to provide them with the necessary opportunities in order to do so.

Rehabilitation first, which would also then protect the public. Also, manage risk.

We should protect the public, especially the vulnerable, and we should seek to rehabilitate the people who commit crimes.

Advise, befriend, assist and protect the public through doing so.

Not surprisingly, respondents also differed in the emphasis placed on various aims, with some concentrating more on rehabilitation and change, while others focused on protection of the public, risk assessment, the enforcement of court orders and licences, and desistance. This reflects the tensions and debates surrounding the purpose of probation work highlighted by Robinson (2008) in relation to discourses focusing on offenders' rights, utilitarian conceptions of rehabilitation and risk management approaches. It suggests that various views on probation work coexisted under a unified service, and it remains to be seen whether some of this diversity will be lost in the new probation set-up:

The aims it had when I first came to work here in 2003 – to protect the public through robust recognition and management of static and dynamic risk factors (many of which come to light through the offender manager–offender working relationship), to ensure the appropriate punishment of offenders within the community, including the enforcement of orders and licences, to work with offenders in their rehabilitation as appropriate.

The Probation Service should be protecting the public. This no longer appears to be its primary objective. It's now fully target-driven with the introduction of meaningless 'SARs' [Specified Activity Requirements] and worthless interventions.

Maybe 'befriend' was not the right word, but probation staff are now automatically linked with police and all about enforcement and punishment. Rehabilitation should be put back at the top of our priorities and not the bottom.

The Probation Service should enshrine, within the heart of the state, the profound perception that people do not stop offending by being punished, by being singled out, demonised and treated differently to others. It should address crime, risk and the plight of offenders and victims from the same perspective, ie, that the community is a whole to which all belong, by right, and that breaches in that wholeness can only be healed when those who made them are persuaded that they still belong and are cared for and can rejoin at any time when they have grown in respect for themselves and others. We should not be protecting the public. That is for the police and prison service. We should be addressing the flaws in society, not in individuals, so that our clients can have lives, as Peter Raynor put it, many years ago, 'in which the rewards of NOT offending are worth having'.

This last quote illustrates a further strain within respondents' thinking about rehabilitation, which is that the underlying problems that individuals face that may lead to offending are as much (if not more) about structural inequalities and injustice as they are about personal issues and 'deficits'. This strain is illustrated well in an article by Collett (2013: 179–80), where he questions the disappearance of class in discussions of probation services and the hijacking of the notion of rehabilitation focused on blaming the individual for their criminal activity.

Respondents also commented about how the service should achieve the various aims set out earlier. Mention was made of the need to continue to develop evidence-based interventions, although there was little mention of what that might entail. There were few references to cognitive behaviourism, which is surprising given its perceived dominance in policy and some areas of practice over the past decade, in particular, following the Effective Practice Initiative (Home Office, 1998), which led to the growth of accredited programmes. Similarly, there is little mention of desistance-based approaches, but, that said, much of the language used about working *with* people to resolve problems, rather than doing things *to* them, may be regarded as using 'desistance language':

> It is well understood from desistance research that without social capital and support, PEOPLE are more likely to offend. No amount of punishment can change that reality. Norway achieves a massive reduction in reoffending by investing realistically in PEOPLE.

> The job of the Probation Service should be about empowering people to change their risky behaviour to improve their own lives and thus reduce the level of harm they cause to individuals and society as a whole.

> To provide rehabilitation services to those who have committed offences. This might involve assisting with practical issues or with cognitive change.

> To assist service users to change destructive patterns of behaviour by motivating them, teaching, mentoring, counselling and challenging them in a supportive way, while helping them to access facilities and opportunities in the wider community so that they can integrate fully.

Moreover, the single most important approach identified by respondents was the skilled professional relationship itself, rather than any particular intervention, and this fits in with the growing number of empirical studies emphasising this phenomenon (Rex, 1999; Raynor, 2004; Burnett and McNeill, 2005; Weaver and McNeill, 2010; King, 2013; Raynor et al, 2013):

> I think we should care for offenders, with staff who are warm as well as wise, and not allowing the sometimes horrible acts undertaken to overwhelm this aim.

> To engage meaningfully with people who commit offences; the service should aim to recruit staff who are able to and encouraged to prioritise the formation of effective working relationships – staff who have a genuine interest in and warmth for other human beings and can help those offenders develop their skills, by getting alongside them, understanding them so that they can be helped to understand themselves better and assisted in identifying and bringing about change in their lives.

> It should be about helping the individual to address the causes of their offending, including their traumatic life and past, their education, employment, their family support, their mental health, etc. It should be about the relationship between the offender and the practitioner.

> To work the majority of our time with service users and victims face-to-face, rather than minimal contact and the majority of the time spent behind a desk at a computer.

> The Probation Service should be trying to reduce reoffending by getting alongside the person, helping them to build links with the community, improve their social capital and family relationships. But, also, it is important to have that protective, preventative role with the majorly high-risk people.

Yes public protection, yes managing risk, lowering reconviction rates, reducing the number of victims, etc, but this is all done by working with offenders. Developing relationships so that we can influence more effectively.

To give people a second chance. To believe in people's ability to change. To treat offenders and victims with respect, as people, not as outsiders from society. To support and care for those no one else wants anything to do with and help them reintegrate into society.

Finally, some respondents made the point that probation work is a difficult job, requiring skill, and one that cannot be done without suitable investment in the workforce, training and qualifications. This raises the issue of levels of qualification and training within the CRCs given that they will not be required to implement the PQF or professionally qualify their workforce under TR (Ministry of Justice, 2013).

The obvious dilemma is that we have a short-term political cycle within which elected politicians seek advantage by appearing to make financial savings and appealing to a misinformed electorate by being 'tough on crime'. However, cutting resources and behaving punitively towards people who have committed offences only increases the likelihood of crime. Perhaps the top priority of the Probation Service, and its most serious failing, is to educate both the electorate and the government sufficiently for them to understand that increased social investment now is more cost-effective than increasing prison places long term, never mind the social misery that could be averted.

Overall, it seems that respondents would want to have a 'business as usual' situation of a unified Probation Service. While this is perhaps not surprising, it does still illustrate the ways in which they were dissatisfied with certain aspects of the old service's overall direction imposed by government, but not with its continuing fundamental purpose, as they felt it should be.

Notes

[1] The difference in agreement between these two statements was not statistically significant.

[2] Responses can exceed a total of 100%. This is because respondents were able to give as many responses as they wished.

4
PROSPECTS FOR THE FUTURE

Protecting the legacy of probation – the new National Probation Service

This chapter discusses respondents' views of the forthcoming (at the time of the survey) organisational changes to probation and the impact that this may have on probation as an ideal, as well as briefly considering the views of a small number of managers who had moved from probation to the private sector. We are still in the midst of dramatic organisational change, but it is clearly unknown as to what levels of collaboration or resistance may occur at an individual level. Indeed, survey responses reflected a deep bitterness over the way in which the changes had been organised and operationalised. Concerns included: working conditions and career prospects; deficiencies in information technology (IT) systems; the implications of low staff morale on working practices and offender engagement; deficiencies in systems set up to manage handovers from a Community Rehabilitation Company (CRC) to the National Probation Service (NPS) and vice versa; and risk assessments and the risks posed by those under probation supervision to the public and probation staff.

It might be surmised that essential elements of the probation ideal will be retained in the NPS despite its shrunken responsibility and size. Previous research suggested that practitioners use a number of strategies to cope with change, including decisions to battle through or even focus on the positives (Robinson and Burnett, 2007: 331; Mawby and Worrall, 2013). Thus, respondents were asked: 'Do you think working for the new National Probation Service would be: better/ worse/no different from working in the existing Probation Service?' Of the respondents who answered the closed question (n = 823), only 33 (4%) felt that working for the new NPS would be better; 702 (85%) felt that it would be worse and 88 (11%) felt that it would be no different. The quantitative responses suggest an overwhelming rejection of the new NPS, which undermined the idea that it could be seen as the continuing symbol of the probation ideal.

Additional comments on this question were made by 90% (n = 739) of respondents who had answered the closed question. At the time of the survey, probation staff had little information of what working for the NPS might entail, and some made comments to that effect. This was seen as a further example of the government treating probation staff with complete disregard by introducing and forcing through 'Transforming Rehabilitation' (TR) changes without properly informing those most affected. This lack of detail would seemingly indicate that the Ministry of Justice, the National Offender Management Service (NOMS) and/or Probation Trust management had been unable or unwilling to provide staff with detailed information, despite this survey being conducted in March/ April 2014, only some four to 10 weeks before the service was split and in the midst of staff being allocated to one of the new organisations. It was not known which of the two organisations our respondents were due to join, although some did comment on their recent allocation.

Under the new TR arrangements, NPS staff complete all court reports and risk assessments and supervise community orders and licences involving 'high risk of harm' individuals, as well as enforcing all breaches. Although many Probation Trusts had previously been divided into teams on similar functional grounds, this division between the NPS and the CRCs was not seen as positive by respondents, as the specialism and division of labour were perceived to be arbitrary, artificial and permanent. This was seen as leading to practitioners within the NPS becoming burdened with an exclusive role of supervising the offenders in the highest risk group. Many felt that this lack of variety and pressure would lead to burnout. There was also some concern about the impact of such a workload upon the service to courts, with a possible increase in Fast Delivery Reports and a consequent reduced level of analysis to assist the court:

> Only high-risk MAPPA [Multi-Agency Public Protection Arrangements] and sex offender work will be very demanding and stressful. It will become more bureaucratic as [part of the] civil service. The caseload is increasing and the loss of lower-risk individuals and especially female offenders will deskill staff.

> The mix of category of risk cases was always very healthy and helpful. I am worried that no risk assessment has been done with regards to staff's health and well-being in dealing with non-stop high-risk stuff.

> No clarity about what the role is but it feels as if all the responsibility will be placed upon the shoulders of NPS staff. There will be constant pressure to get assessments right, these will come back to bite them when anything goes wrong in the CRC, eg, an SFO [serious further offence]. The job will be a relentless round of risk assessment and MAPPA meetings and supervising risky individuals. There will be no downtime with low-/medium-risk individuals who just need a bit of guidance on sorting themselves out. Instead, it will be just worry, worry, worry.

Objections were made to the likely increase in work and the changing nature of supervision due to such increases. Respondents made comments about a shortage of staff, which would increase pressure, leading to stress and sickness absences, which itself would then feed a vicious circle. The increase in workload was seen as coming from the CRCs possibly 'exaggerating' risk and trying to offload more risky cases as this would increase the chances of successful outcomes for their caseload.

Many respondents felt that the nature of their work would change and that they would substantively become case managers, as opposed to probation officers able to undertake 'offending work' with their supervisees. Respondents envisaged a future of report writing, case recording and risk assessment, with the rehabilitative part of their work gone. Thus, they felt that they would be 'protecting the public' in a narrow administrative sense. While this has come to be accepted by practitioners over recent decades as an important aspect of their work, probation staff in a number of research studies have held on to 'people work' and have seen rehabilitation with even the higher-risk individuals as at least as important as risk management in reducing risk and protecting the public (Annison et al, 2008; Deering, 2011; Mawby and Worrall, 2013). Furthermore, the anticipated loss of face-to-face work was viewed very negatively as this has consistently been reported as fundamentally important to practitioners in terms of job satisfaction (and as one of the main reasons for joining the service) and vital in terms of successful outcomes for supervision (Annison et al, 2008; Deering, 2011; Raynor et al, 2013):

> My feelings are that NPS staff will be more chained to their computers than currently. Dealing with high-risk offenders only will mean, in my opinion, less face-to-face contact. I can see the jobs being purely report writing and OASys [Offender Assessment System] assessments often on people we have never met.

> The probability is that staff will be stuck in work silos and will eventually burn out – it will be public protection only and not 'as well as rehabilitation' – therefore they will be deskilled.

> Working with high-risk only needs intensive supervision and support; there is no indication that this will be available. There is no indication that the new NPS is value-based. Could be offender management only, more bureaucratic, form filling, targets, sat all day in front of a computer screen, not enough time to actually talk

to people and make meaningful interventions. Could be all about enforcement and control rather than rehabilitation.

I fear I [am] doomed to become a risk assessment tool monkey. Little flexibility and minimised time working with clients making a difference. Apart from adding to and narrowing the workload, the split was also seen a causing a loss of knowledge and expertise to both the NPS and the CRCs, and it was anticipated that communication between the two would not be free, open and effective due to the split itself and to the privatised nature of the CRCs. This was seen as problematic for the NPS per se, but particularly perhaps in the case of possible of risk management and the danger of offenders committing SFOs:

> Because of the split with CRC, a lot of skills and knowledge will be lost.

> Loss of information. From now on, whether you are in CRC or NPS as a case manager, you will not be able to call up the details on all the relevant individuals you might like to know about or to discuss their situations with the supervising officers as part of one team. Good case management requires joined-up teamwork. Although in terms of my work, being an offender manager may not significantly change, what will is the disjointed [nature] and fragmentation of services. This in turn will impact upon communication with others and the sharing of important information.

> No idea on how to transfer cases or communicate with CRCs – just a mess. I have absolutely no confidence in NPS.

> I think the way the caseload is to be divided between two providers will be chaos and will lead to very serious further incidents. I think that the stress on staff on both sides will be appalling, the confusion for service users unhelpful and the system will be a total mess.

The artificial split makes no sense in relation to what we know about when SFOs happen – ie, information sharing, consistent decision-making, etc. My presumption is that the notion of rehabilitation will be preserved for the medium- and low-risk and the rights of the 'high-risk' as citizens will be ignored.

NPS will end up being gatekeepers for CRC enforcement and risk assessments. There will be vast additional processes that will cost time and waste public monies, which may also place the public at risk.

Many respondents commented negatively on the impact of becoming a civil servant and not a single positive comment was made in that regard. The civil service was seen as less flexible, more bureaucratic and far more demanding of its staff in terms of conformity to government policy and diktat, and respondents felt that they would lose a degree of autonomy and thus be required to 'do the bidding' of the Ministry of Justice, rather than act in the traditional role of the independent officer of the court, offering analysis and advice. The NPS was seen as likely to operate with a Prison Service 'command and control mentality', and thus the removal of the Trusts would strip away a 'buffer' between practitioners, offenders and the politicised state. The anticipated monolithic nature of the NPS would be reinforced by its size, with only seven divisions covering the whole of England and Wales and, with the exception of Wales and London, all would be coterminous with more than one CRC:

I think becoming the equivalent to a civil servant (without any of the obvious benefits) is likely to result in a more rigid, inflexible, bureaucratic and risk-averse organisation than at present.

Seems to be prison command and control model from emails, etc, I have seen so far – not suitable for our work and demoralising for staff to be handed sets of instructions for doing a job we have been doing well for years. I don't want to be constrained by being a civil servant – at my grievance hearing, they couldn't tell me whether I can continue campaigning on issues outside of work or not.

We don't have enough information to date, but I would be concerned that working for the civil service, our autonomy and independence as practitioners would be lost.

Even more rigid and bureaucratic since there is no longer going to be the buffer of the Trusts between the workers and the Ministry. The tradition of the civil service will weigh heavily and there will be moves towards severe cost/staff cutting here as well, with workers overburdened by large caseloads consisting of the most violent and dangerously damaged people, no light relief.

There is a significant culture shift in becoming a civil servant, not all good by the look of it. The Probation Service is diverse and not frightened by challenge and a dissenting voice. I am not so sure that will be acceptable within the civil service.

However, a small minority of those who responded were positive about the potential for change, in part, based on/reflecting what they saw as the negative side of the Probation Service, although this is perhaps qualified by an assessment of the changes to the service immediately preceding TR:

The current service does not have a clear identity and I suspect that is very much linked to the reducing budgets over the years, overly high workloads, the threats of privatisation and the last 24 months of uncertainty solely at the hands of Mr Grayling. The service is fragmented and I believe exhausted. A clear start with clear expectations is what I am anticipating – if this happens, however, is to be seen.

Far better. It will be more accountable, transparent and less nepotistic than existing Probation Trusts.

I hope it will be a more respected role – probation officers can become leaders in public protection and rehabilitation of high risk offenders.

More broadly, reflecting on different empirical studies that tracked the impact of the many changes to probation on probation staff, a sense emerges that the probation profession may continue to attract the same and the 'right' kind of people but that they may well increasingly suffer from the distance between organisational and policy expectations and personal values. This may be expected to be particularly painful for those working for private, profit-making organisations. However, in our previous exploratory study with probation managers who had moved to the private sector, we found that respondents were able to protect their personal 'probation' values by reframing their employers' profit needs as conducive to producing good and ethical working practices. Two comments illustrated this point:

this assertion that the private sector is driven by profit is – I'm not sure if that's right ... you run a project so that you can achieve both, that you can achieve the ethos and the goals and you can do it more cheaply ... if you were to go up to the head offices of G4S or Serco or whatever and find out what drives people there, making a profit for the shareholders doesn't really enter [into] it ... it's things like ... will I stay in favour with my boss ... will I still be in a job in a year's time?... I'm sure the accountants in the head office are very much aware of the need for shareholders to get a dividend, but they'll know that – they – they would prefer – they want to renew the contract as well ... what drives you is wanting to be successful and therefore keep your job. (Deering et al, 2014: 243)

I kind of can justify my existence in the private sector because I still have what some people would determine to be public sector values but they're, you know, they are perfectly applicable within the private sector. (Deering et al, 2014: 243)

Similarly, in a small study on electronic monitoring officers working for private sector companies, Hucklesby (2013: 152) noted that they appeared to share some values and a sense of mission in relation to their responsibility of monitoring offenders. Some ($n = 7$) of the 20 monitoring officers participating in Hucklesby's research displayed 'probation worker' values: displaying empathy and a heightened level of trust in offenders; treating offenders with respect; and demonstrating adherence to ideals of procedural justice. Half of the participating officers were characterised as pragmatists, holding non-judgemental attitudes towards offenders and being concerned primarily with completing their work efficiently and effectively. A small minority of monitoring officers ($n = 3$) were described as technicians, who had no sympathy for offenders and were highly suspicious of them, keeping engagement with offenders to a minimum. Hucklesby (2013: 156) concludes that how monitoring officers go about their work is 'not sector-specific but is dictated by the working environment'. These two small studies into private sector values (among managers and practitioners in different job roles) towards offenders might suggest that, at the very least, former probation staff within the CRCs will find their new employment environment to be challenging and complex in terms of retaining their professional values.

Collaboration between the National Probation Service and Community Rehabilitation Companies – mending a broken relationship?

Early discussions of the proposed split of probation into two separate organisations were concerned with how communication and handover between these organisations would be managed. So, in addition, respondents were asked about their views on 'What issues might be important in the relationship between the National Probation Service and the Community Rehabilitation Companies?'.

This was an open question only and comments were received from 766 respondents (58% of the total sample). Of immediate interest was the fact that many respondents did not directly answer the question posed, but used it to express their feelings about TR generally. Those who did this were exclusively opposed to TR and expressed this opposition in terms that showed their anger, frustration and feelings of helplessness and betrayal at the part-privatisation of the service and the split into two organisations, which was seen as arbitrary, divisive, professionally disastrous and liable to make rehabilitation and the protection of the public far more difficult to achieve. In short, these changes were seen as increasing the risk of reoffending and highly injurious to staff morale:

> NOMS is not listening to experienced probation staff or inspectors – the impression is more that existing staff and services are regarded with contempt by government. All those who can are therefore leaving. Those who can't leave now are planning how to exit from probation as quickly as possible. If the country were not in such an economic downturn, I think the exodus of staff would already have paralysed the service nationally; the difficulties of achieving full staff establishment in London are evidence in support. The TR changes are only going ahead because the majority of the current workforce feels trapped or captive, without short-term options. I can see no commitment to making TR work below senior management grades. From where I sit at the coalface of the new NPS, it currently appears far more likely that probation services will break down and fail entirely than that they will 'work' or 'succeed' under TR. If/ when it all goes wrong, probation staff anticipate that NOMS will look for scapegoats at the operational level. Coalface staff already feel seriously unsupported. If staff do not leave entirely, stress-related absence may add to operational failures.

In September 2014, Napo and the public service trade union UNISON published a survey in which 80% of respondents stated that they had considered leaving their job and 55% said that they were actively looking for a new job (Lezard, 2014). This clearly echoes sentiments in responses to our questions:

Morale. It's naive to think that staff divided by screens can work together. In [names Trust], morale is rock-bottom. People are losing interest in their work with a 'What's the point?' attitude growing within the service. A service that once prided itself on quality work.

In all honesty, the relationship in my office and those of colleagues I know around the country, between CRC- and NPS-delegated staff is deteriorating rapidly and the change has not yet occurred.

There is a feeling of injustice from those moving to the CRCs and many of those that are moving have ceased engaging in shared roles with NPS staff, do not even engage in polite conversation and have stopped performing their roles to the same standard – disappointingly, this is also being seen from team managers, who have the attitude 'I won't be here in a month, so not my problem'. One has even stated 'I'm not countersigning OASys anymore'.

Some of the previous comments suggest that there was grave concern in relation to a complete breakdown of the relationship between NPS and CRC staff, many of whom were still located in the same buildings. Comments also highlighted the dangers for public safety in cases where professionalism might give way to short-term self-interest. It remains to be seen whether this will reflect wider trends among a possibly disaffected workforce.

When addressing the question more directly, respondents showed a very high degree of homogeneity and agreement, both in the issues that they identified as pertinent in the relationship between the NPS and CRCs and in how these issues might unfold in the new structures. Chief among these was communication, the sharing of data and information, and the concern that important information about risk was likely to be lost, interpreted in different ways by the two organisations or otherwise compromised. At a basic level, communication between two organisations was inevitably seen as going to be slower and potentially less effective, exacerbated by lack of access to IT and record-keeping and complicated assessment systems, such as OASys and Delius:

> Communication will be a big one. Here's a little example and we don't officially change over yet! My manager was on leave last week, so I asked the usual manager who fills in when he is off to authorise some leave I needed and to countersign a PSR [Pre-Sentence Report] – much delay, then told I need to go to an NPS manager not a CRC manager.

> To be effective, there needs to be good communication between the two organisations – it is hard to see how this will be achieved within the current structures.

> Clear communication, common/shared target times for sharing information, clear understanding of each agency's role. In all honesty, the relationship in my office and those of colleagues I know around the country between CRC- and NPS-delegated staff is deteriorating rapidly and the change has not yet occurred.

> The interface between the two will become a chasm. Cases will fall betwixt and between. The focus will be on competition not cooperation.

> Data – use of Delius/OASys – can the two organisations share the same data?

The Her Majesty's Inspectorate of Probation (HMIP, 2014) report on the early stages of TR and a Napo (2015) briefing on its impact seem to confirm these concerns, referring to four main issues of implementation: major problems with the IT systems in the NPS and CRCs; significant staff shortages in many areas, with a reliance on agency staff; high workloads; and safeguarding issues due to communication problems between the NPS and CRCs (HMIP, 2014b; Napo, 2015; see also Leftly, 2014a, 2014b). Practically, competition between different CRC providers – regardless to which sector they belong – will likely make information sharing contentious, potentially business-sensitive and covered by commercial confidentiality, and thus vital to securing future funding. As a result, a significant aspect of the NPS and CRCs working together to manage risk may thus be undermined by the very instruments introduced to improve service delivery, namely, contestability and marketisation.

Communication and relationships were seen as problematic in general, but especially in terms of 'higher risk of harm' individuals, or those individuals where risk was escalating and might involve the possibility of SFOs; several respondents pointed out that enquiries into the latter invariably referred to poor communication. It was seen as pretty much inevitable that such communication would be even poorer between two organisations compared to a single entity and that this would be magnified by the ways in which these organisations had been created, were constituted and were likely to operate. Questions of communication were overlaid by issues of trust, commercial confidentiality, data protection and so on, and there was concern expressed that staff in the two organisations would increasingly see themselves as separate, with different interests, particularly as it has already become clear that access to records and information held by the 'other side' may be difficult (HMIP, 2014; Napo, 2015; Leftly, 2014a, 2014b):

> Common understanding of risk and risk escalation. Important, that CRCs retain suitably probation-qualified staff equality, ie, NPS should not become the more senior/important organisation.

As far as I am aware, I have been told that NPS are not allowed to share any information about their cases with the CRC. In a series of reviews conducted on cases who have committed serious further offences, one factor that is always present when there has been a failure in case management is lack of communication between different agencies.

A shared set of values and understanding of need and risk. An undertaking to share information re risk and need, eg, male high-risk DV [domestic violence] offender in NPS begins relationship with a low-risk female in CRC. Information needs shared!!

Duplicating work! Inconsistency between the two services in the way they manage things, giving out unclear messages to our service users. Fragmentation of communication and services. People getting 'lost in the system' when they pass between the two, or offender managers no longer being able to build rapport with their cases, and cases who move between medium and high risk will flit between the two services.

Communication!! For two separate organisations to function, there has to be lots of interface. It's been proven through SFOs time and time again that communication is the one thing that fails between organisations, and is likely to again if risk of cases is not properly discussed or if info regarding offenders is not passed over.

H[erschel] Prinz, 'All tragedy is a failure of communication'.

Moreover, the CRCs were regarded as becoming seen as inferior in terms of the importance of their work and the training and status of their staff, and that this would be compounded by them being the passive recipients of cases assessed as lower risk by NPS staff. This 'them and us' situation (in addition to the 'them and us' of management and practitioners) was mentioned by many respondents and was a clear theme in the responses to this particular issue. Indeed, many respondents were of the view that this shift to a 'them and us' mentality had already happened, or was beginning to happen at the time of the survey in March/April 2014, shortly before the actual split at the end of May 2014. There was agreement that the corrosive effects of this had begun to influence staff locally, despite this being between staff who were still employed by one organisation and who had, until that point, been colleagues, some for a considerable period of time. This was seen as inevitably becoming a bigger divide as time goes on, as staff change and as the links with previous colleagues begin to dissipate:

> CRC seen as poor relation and junior partner, people working within the CRC seen as less [important] – not an issue? It's already happening.

> There needs to be sensitivity – qualified staff who are used to making decisions relating to risk will now have to gain 'NPS' approval, which is both insulting and demoralising.

> The 'us and them' mentality has already begun – and we've barely got started. If the MoJ [Ministry of Justice] think that we will be working together in harmony as one big happy family, they've got another thing coming!

> [Hopefully,] it doesn't become them and us. I have been on the other side and it is not nice. We are all good at what we do and should have been kept together. However, experience tells me relationships will inevitably change for the worse. How sad.

> The fact that the minister keeps referring to the NPS as a team of specialist staff [is not helpful] when, in fact, the split has come about through a very random process for staff and the same experienced staff will be in the CRC, some of which will be better qualified and skilled than those in the NPS.

> Through the whole process of the split, the staff who have been allocated to the CRC have been made to feel that they will not be as valued as their colleagues in the NPS. This will and has created negative feelings, which will not help working relationships.

> NPS seen as some kind of 'elite'. NPS caseloads will become higher/ more stressful and CRCs [will be] blamed for this.

Them and us: an elitist NPS and a second-rate CRC.

The preceding sentiments will likely be compounded by the requirement upon the NPS to employ professionally qualified staff, but the reduced requirement on CRCs to only have staff 'suitably' trained, with no reference to professional or educational standards or benchmarks (Ministry of Justice, 2013). Differences here will inevitably be exacerbated over time as fewer CRC staff are likely to be professionally qualified. These issues were seen as making a two-tier system inevitable, with a clear hierarchy of status and importance evolving:

> I think professional respect will be an issue as those officers going to the CRC are feeling deskilled. Having worked for the Prison Service, I am very aware of the lack of respect from both staff and prisoners towards private sector staff – they are not deemed to be 'real' prison officers.

> The quality/qualifications of workers in the CRC will gradually diminish and snobbishness may become evident in NPS towards CRC workers. It is implied in the split that CRC workers will not be competent in managing risk and cannot be trusted to maintain quality.

> Initially, staff will be immediate colleagues who understand both areas of work. BUT this will gradually change and experience of working with all offenders and various aspects of probation will decline and create a less aware and widely skilled workforce, and knowledge will be lost as the opportunities are narrowed. POs/PSOs [Probation Officers/Probation Service Officers] in CRCs [will] become deskilled in risk work.

> Mutual respect – I am concerned that over time, in the NPS, historic probation staff will be replaced with inexperienced civil servants who do not have the same value base or skills with offenders as

traditional probation staff, and that in the CRC, experienced staff will eventually be replaced with cheaper, less experienced and unqualified staff, or experienced staff will be treated without any respect for their experience and judgement by non-probation-experience civil servants.

In the longer run, NPS staff may raise questions as to the legitimacy of CRC staff working with offenders 'for profit' in a competition to maintain status and significance. This is likely to contaminate communication between the two organisations, and many respondents felt that such communication is likely to be made more problematic by differing organisational agendas. These agendas are driven by the need of the CRCs to be 'successful' in reoffending terms, which may encourage them to overemphasise levels of risk of harm in order to move potentially problematic, or less compliant, individuals to the NPS. Payment by Results (PbR) contracts and the need for the CRCs to be profitable may make this inevitable, and recent controversies and fraud investigations involving private sector companies' handling of criminal justice service contracts do lend some support to such suspicions.[1]

In more general terms, the split was seen as inevitably skewing the work of both organisations and destroying the value base of 'probation work', resulting in a fundamental change in its nature:

> The undermining of the professionalism of the Probation Service; reducing the variety and scope of probation work, which used to make it interesting, enjoyable and doable; the need to make a profit for shareholders will have a detrimental effect on the viability of work with offenders.

> Maintaining a focus on risk rather than contract detail.

> The individual needs to know they are person, not a commodity – retaining the dignity and humanity elements.

Differing objectives – especially if CRCs become profit-making …
and PbR comes into play – will potentially affect working relations.

CRCs will 'cherry-pick' work and risk will be assessed accordingly.
Unlikeable or non-compliant challenging people will be more
likely to be deemed high-risk and sent to NPS, superficially 'easy'
people will be kept.

CRCs will skew figures to give a better account of performance (It
happens now in some Trusts, so why not afterwards?).

There will never be a good relationship. How can the two marry
when one is motivated by money and profit from some of the
most vulnerable people in society? What professional ethics will
CRCs have?

Finally, although initial risk assessments and case allocation will be
carried out by the NPS (NOMS, 2014a), there was some confusion
over the movement of cases between the organisations. Some
respondents noted the initial position that, once supervised by the
NPS, cases could not return to the CRC, even if risk of harm has
clearly reduced. While the process of risk escalation was clarified in
October 2014 by NOMS (2014b), the process of transferring cases
back from the NPS to CRCs once risk has reduced remains unclear
at the current time (January/February 2015).

If you could change the world …

We also wished to consider respondent views of an idealised delivery
of probation services. Therefore, respondents were asked to suggest
some ideas thus: 'If you were starting with a blank sheet, how would
you organise community supervision in terms of a public/private/
third sector balance?'. About half of respondents (651), answered
this question. There seemed to be considerable agreement that the
core responsibility should lie with the public sector, the Probation

Service. However, there was considerably less agreement on what the appropriate role would be for the third and private sectors. While some respondents did not wish to see any private or third sector involvement, some suggested that both sectors had an important role to play in supporting probation work:

> I wouldn't consider the private and third sector as there is too much of a lack of accountability.

> 100% public as I believe that all offending/risk work should remain within the public sector and control of the government. Working with offenders should not be about profit; people are not products, but individuals and one size does not fit all.

> I wouldn't organise it in that way. I simply don't understand how, morally, justice/punishment/rehabilitation can be seen to be delivered by anyone other than a state organisation which is held accountable to the public.

Some of those who supported the involvement of other sectors did specify 'appropriate' roles for the third and the private sector; others were less specific:

> Public sector offender management and a mixed supply chain of private, public and third sector intervention providers being commissioned by the offender management on basis of cost and effectiveness.

Some respondents were unwilling to make any suggestions as to the 'right' balance, reflecting bitterness over the status of probation, or suggested alternative approaches to community supervision:

> Ask Mr Grayling. He seems to know all the answers.

Invest in restorative justice processes; communities to take responsibility for their own people rather than annex them to the prison estate.

To put it simply: extend IOM [Integrated Offender Management] practice to the whole of community supervision. It costs a lot of money but it works. I would find the money by getting rid of NOMS and restricting short-term prison sentences and then reallocating the funds from NOMS and prisons to probation.

Small workers' cooperatives contracted by a National Probation Service.

Some comments reflected on the fundamental question of whether it matters which sector delivers community supervision, with a clear focus on the characteristics of the individuals carrying out community supervision, for example, the level of training and commitment. Of course, it is unclear whether levels of training will remain the same in CRCs, and they will only have to provide suitable and appropriate levels of training (Ministry of Justice, 2013):

For me, I do not think it is a question of who does what, it is a question of ensuring that the people working within the organisations are appropriately trained and skilled to do the job and are paid a fair wage to do so.

A significant proportion of responses suggested a preference for a system of community supervision exclusively run by the public sector. Comments overall, however, reflected an appreciation of the need for anyone involved in community supervision to work in partnership; indeed, there were numerous references to partnership (75) in the comments. Comments reflected on the significant extent of partnership work in existence prior to TR, and, in the main, partnership was constructed as the public sector commissioning services from the third or private sector:

I would have had the statutory body at the centre but maybe introduced competition (if we must use that word) in the provision of partnership work on projects and programmes. Many excellent projects have been developed in partnerships in the past, such as CJDT [Criminal Justice Drugs Team] and REACH [a structured day programme for people with drug and/or alcohol misuse issues], but they will now be part of the CRCs and this has put them in a tenuous position with the commissioners. Why mend what wasn't broken. Best practice could have been taken from around the country and explored to see if could be developed in different localities.

I don't think it is right that anyone should be allowed to profit from crime and offending and I think issues like the tagging scandals only reinforce this. I believe that supervision of offenders and other aspects of criminal justice should remain within the state. That is not to say, however, that there is no role at all for private/ third sector organisations. As indicated before, they provide some great services in areas like housing, mental health, substance use etc and can be invaluable as, with high caseloads, it's not possible to do all this work with every case. I do think it should be done in partnership, however, rather than them having sole management.

I would have the Probation Trusts as they are and I would encourage or provide avenues for better partnership and multi-agency working between probation and local charities and agencies. Sole responsibility for risk management and enforcement would remain with the Probation Service.

It is thus clear that most respondents felt that the provision of community supervision should remain within the public sector, and that many were open to partnership work, including work with the private sector, but that this should not include transfer of risk management to the private sector.

Perspectives on legitimacy – who should do 'probation work'?

Following on from idealised visions of Probation Service provision, the issue of legitimacy, of who *should* do the work, arises. The legitimacy of other aspects of criminal justice, in particular, that of policing practices, and questions over outsourcing aspects of criminal justice and penal processes to the private sector have been debated over the past decade or so (see Tyler, 2006; Hough et al, 2010). Legitimacy has been defined as the 'property of an authority … that leads people to feel that that authority … is entitled to be deferred to and obeyed' (Sunshine and Tyler, 2003: 513). The privatisation of criminal justice services raises fundamental normative questions about the ethics of private companies making a profit from crime, victimisation and punishment. Despite this, in England and Wales, there seems no longer to be a broad-based debate about the legitimacy of privatisation of punishment (if there ever was one) and there is a scarcity of research about whether 'sector matters' for internal legitimacy (that felt by those subjected to punishment) or external legitimacy (that felt by the audience not directly affected by punishment).[2]

In relation to probation, it is as yet unclear how those under the supervision of the NPS and CRCs will respond to the change in ownership and whether it will matter to them in terms of compliance with their orders and licence arrangements. In relation to the legitimacy of those delivering community sentences, Sunshine and Tyler's (2003) definition cited earlier would suggest that privatisation could affect offenders' perception of legitimacy. For example, Jackson et al (2010) discuss how the legitimacy of specific prison regimes is affected by a number of factors, including procedural justice, but also perceived motivations of those imposing punishment. They suggest that:

> People are influenced by their inferences about the motivations of the authorities with whom they are dealing. If people feel that authorities are acting out of a sincere desire to do what is right, then they view the authorities as acting more fairly. If people think

> that an authority is not concerned about their well-being then they
> react negatively to its actions. (Jackson et al, 2010: 10)

Furthermore, as discussed earlier, many commentators suggest that effective probation work is premised on the nature of the relationship between offender and practitioner, and, thus, the relationship may be the 'key site or resource within which to develop legitimacy' (McNeill and Robinson, 2013: 122). However, in relation to compliance with the electronic monitoring of curfews, Hucklesby (2013: 148) found that none of the offenders interviewed 'questioned the legitimacy of monitoring officers as representatives of a private company'. Thus, in general terms, the relatively limited literature on the subject suggests that few conclusions can yet be drawn about whether 'ownership' is clearly linked to internal legitimacy.

The focus in this report is elsewhere, however. TR has highlighted another, important, dimension to legitimacy, namely, the extent to which those who are administering punishment on behalf of the state view their own practices and those of others in the system as legitimate. In this sense, we asked our respondents for their views on a number of related aspects of legitimacy, for example, the importance of who is involved in probation work and the implications for those under probation supervision. We asked a closed question on whether respondents felt that it mattered 'who does probation as long as it was done well'. Respondents were quite unequivocal in their verdict. Out of 790 responses, 71% felt that it did matter, 17% that it did not and 12% were undecided; 628 respondents commented further on this issue.

Some respondents felt that the question had been ill-defined and was therefore difficult to answer. In many respects, these comments reflect a wider lack of clarity over what would qualify as 'good probation work'. It is a reflection of the struggle over the term 'rehabilitation', as well as the wider value base of probation work beyond utilitarian rehabilitation, as discussed earlier. Comments clearly made distinctions between meeting targets and believing in a rights-based approach to offenders:

But it depends on the definition of quality.

It entirely depends on your definition of 'well'. The work needs to be underpinned by the fundamental belief that justice is the responsibility of the state.

What does 'it is done well' mean? Are we judging this solely on results – ie, lack of reoffending or making a real change to individuals?

It is well known the Probation Service has achieved its targets but the issue is: is what is being asked relevant and appropriate? The question begs what is probation work aiming to do. Doing something well does not mean that it is the right thing to be doing. Also, is doing it well to include within budget and is this an annual budget or lifetime budget for the individual or society?

Of course it matters. Would you want me operating on your sick granny so long as I kinda 'did it well'?

That assumes private sector and other providers are capable of doing a job, which does not seem possible to me. Values are essential to our work, for example, for role modelling, treating our cases as valued individuals not like a sausage factory. Positive relationships with their worker are what are found to be most effective in reducing reoffending. This is labour-intensive, with workers needing to have time to work with offenders, including time to plan sessions and work with other agencies.

'Done well' is subjective. 'Done well' for whom, the offender? The public? The shareholders?

Those delivering this work need to be free from the pressures of profit and focused on offering good risk management and support to those individuals. Probation has to be accountable not to shareholders, but to society as a whole.

I think the public – if little known – face of staff who work with offenders needs to be 'professional' to engender confidence in our work. A public sector organisation that everyone is paying into, and thereby taking some responsibility for how we treat offenders at even a very distant level, is important so that society sees it does have some responsibility to this group of its citizens.

Importantly, unprompted, many respondents ($n = 218$; 35%) explicitly highlighted their moral qualms about 'making profit' from crime, and others made reference to the importance of public accountability. We have selected a few pertinent comments in the following. This normative opposition to allowing profiting from crime resonates with Crewe and Liebling (2012b). In their study on the views on privatisation of senior managers in the prison system, half of the senior managers reported being strongly ideologically opposed to private prisons on the basis that punishment should be a function of the state (Crewe and Liebling, 2012b: 26). However, experiences of the improvements of prison standards as a result of privatisation seemed to overrule managers' normative concerns in the longer term. Perhaps a distinction here between prisons and probation is that there did seem to be a level of consensus over the past decades that public sector prisons needed to improve (Crewe and Liebling, 2012b: 26), while this was far less clearly the case regarding probation. One of the arguments put forward by government for marketisation and privatisation was the alleged lack of creativity in probation practice and the continuation of high reoffending rates for individuals on community orders and licences (Clarke, 2010; Ministry of Justice, 2011, 2012, 2013). However, this was counterbalanced by reports pointing out the effectiveness and efficiency of the Probation Service in a number of areas.[3] In any event, respondents showed themselves to be strongly opposed to privatisation:

See above for the moral argument about the deliverance of justice and the importance of being impartial. If we worked for a company that was subsequently convicted for criminal matters, that would make us part of a criminal organisation. It would be akin to the mafia delivering justice. It would be farcical even if we did our jobs well.

Justice is a public good. Justice is done by the state and through communities, and so anyone involved in this process should be responsible to the communities and not operating for financial reasons.

The public sector is not for profit, has ethos and a dedicated set of people who came into this work out of a commitment to what they do. I could give countless examples where people I work with have spent hours completing reports or doing work to protect the public and assist their clients, often putting their hands in their own pockets and offering their time and assistance when there is nothing or no one else to help them. The service has experience that is unparalleled by the third or private sector. Why should there be a need to complicate and confuse what exists with inferior alternatives. You will not get this dedication and service in a private company that drives down costs by reducing salaries, terms and conditions and standards of training for those it employs, whose sole interest is profit for shareholders and senior personnel. We are not in the business of packing fruit, but that's what it could become. There are too few not-for-profit organisations and their interests are too narrow in focus to complete the tasks we do with public protection and working with individuals to improve their lives. I do strongly believe that there is a need for public services that act to improve the lives of their clients and protect the public. That is why probation should remain untouched by short-term, economic ideologues with no real interest or experience.

Offenders are amongst the most deprived sections of society and it is immoral for anyone to make a profit out of them. There is also a conflict of interest for the private sector in that if they succeed in reducing reoffending, they might deprive themselves of work– does anyone really think that this is realistic?

People who commit offences need to be seen as humans not cash cows. It's not hard to understand.

Respondents also referred to the effects of the privatisation of probation on both internal and external legitimacy. Additionally, when discussing the dangers of introducing a profit motive, reference was made to the level of problems/misadministration and outright corruption witnessed in the US, as well as concerns over the practices of private sector companies delivering criminal justice services in England and Wales:

Public confidence. Justice is by the people for the people. Nation needs to have confidence in the system, fairness and equity for all. Accountability. Other examples of private probation systems in other countries (ie USA) are not good. Justice must not be driven by a profit motive.

Criminal justice should never be about profit. You only need to look at what is happening in America where they own prisons, they charge offenders for tags and then if they cannot pay, they are returned to court. That would appear to be the way we are heading.

We have proven we do a good job. Working with offenders should remain within the public services in order to maintain service delivery to a high standard. We are part of the justice system and accountable to government. If privatised, we would be open to corruption for payment. Look at America.

The examples of 'doing it well' come from the Probation Service; yes, improvements can always be made but [the] current system does not need dismantling to achieve better results. [The] American model shows that once profit-making companies become involved, the system does not improve offenders' lives – or reduce costs for the taxpayer!

It should be driven by public service, not profit. This is not a product/commodity, it's about people's lives, liberty and security; this should not be bought and sold like a loaf of bread. There have already been reports of major problems with private sector companies in the criminal justice system, eg, tagging, interpreting services, delivering prisoners to court, management of prisons, according to reports in the press/media. This is not just a recent problem, but seems to be worsening.

Other comments on this question related to concerns over the practical implications and dangers of the fragmentation of the service:

The fact remains that the existing service does it well and there is no evidence to suggest that fragmenting the service will make it any better, we believe it will be to the detriment of the current good practice. I accept that there is always room for improvement but we need some evidence to convince us that the governments restructure will do that.

Should be done by one organisation, whether that be private or public; however, splitting it is the worst-case scenario.

There need to be legal and ethical boundaries between agencies. Probation has a proven track record and it is unethical to make profit or make an industry out of probation work. However, some private companies are obviously proven to be highly ethical and would make welcome partners, I would have thought. Third sector intervention, eg, drug programmes, are arguably in some areas better than probation-equivalent, which adds to an argument against probation monopolising work with offenders.

While there were few comments supporting the notion that the 'who' delivers does not matter as long as the work is done well, some respondents recognised that there may be alternative ways of providing probation, with the important caveat that TR was not the way to do it. Additionally, there was a clear message as to the importance of consistent training and the supervision of staff:

> Ultimately, if it is being done well and risk of harm managed appropriately along with the rehabilitative side of things, then that is fine; however, I do not believe that TR is the way forward for this.

> To do well it surely needs qualified staff. It is a profession that should be protected.

> Not really – the word 'probation' has now lost the meaning it used to have, it's already not the same thing it was anyway. It doesn't matter who does it – but the values of the organisation that does it IS important. However, it is entirely wrong to suggest that a profit-making organisation will put the needs of the person in front of them ahead of their cost margin/profit.

> Probation work has to be carried out by properly trained and supervised probation staff.

In addition to the questions previously discussed, we posed four attitudinal statements in relation to the importance of the nature of the organisation – as in public sector, private sector or third sector – that delivers probation and offender management services. These questions and responses are listed in Table 4.1. We reversed some of the statements to test consistency and found significant agreement across different questions: 70% of those who agreed that legitimacy is important to compliance also agreed that compliance in practice is likely affected by supervision by private or third sector organisations ($p < 0.000$). Similarly, 79% of those who agreed that punishment

Table 4.1: Attitudinal statements relating to legitimacy

Question	Strongly Agree	Agree	Neither Agree nor Disagree	Disagree	Strongly Disagree	Responses
It is important in terms of compliance that individuals on supervision see the organisation supervising them as legitimate	85%	13%	1%	–	–	795
Punishment (including community sentences and licences) should only be delivered by agencies of the state	77%	15%	5%	2%	1%	795
Offenders are less likely to comply with orders if they are supervised by private and/ or third sector organisations	35%	35%	25%	5%	1%	795
It does not matter who delivers community orders as long as the service is of a good quality	2%	11%	12%	32%	44%	794

should only be delivered by the state disagreed that it does not matter who delivers community orders ($p < 0.000$).

In our previous pilot study, managers who had chosen to move from the public sector to the private sector had justified the profit motive of private sector organisations with reference to the quality of service provision. The argument was that the private sector saw quality of service as the best method to ensure continued profits and the ability to win contracts (Deering et al, 2014). Recognising the fundamental difference between those who chose to move into the private sector and the respondents in this research who were about to be forced into a new organisation, we posed an attitudinal statement about whether respondents felt that private sector organisations would see the provision of a quality service as the best way to make a profit. Less than a quarter (22%; $n = 173$) of all respondents ($n = 788$) agreed with this statement; a clear majority of 70% disagreed with the statement and 8% were undecided. There was a small difference between managers (75%) and practitioners (71%) responding to this question. Finally, a minority of our respondents felt that it should not matter to which sector an organisation delivering probation services 'belonged':

> Good work and best practice are always important. I don't really mind who pays me provided the service is good and risk is managed appropriately.

> If the work is being done effectively, why should it matter who is doing it? Beyond performance, ultimately, any concerns that staff have are purely selfish and are regarding their pay, terms and conditions. It is understandable for those who have worked in the service many years and have dedicated their careers to a profession where they have expected to receive certain terms and conditions of service, who now find these factors at risk. However, more long term, new employees will know what they are signing up for.

It is important to emphasise again that our survey was completed by a self-selected, mainly Napo-affiliated, sample of probation staff. This particular group of respondents was clearly fundamentally opposed to the splitting up of the Probation Service and its part-privatisation. How much, or for how long, these normative objections can survive the reality of working within the private sector is unknown. As mentioned, Crewe and Liebling (2012b: 26) noted that, over time, a form of 'pragmatic acceptance' set in among those exposed to privatisation in the prison sector, acknowledging the existence of good-quality private prisons and a general driving up of standards. In the eyes of senior prison managers, moral arguments lost out to considerations of 'quality, effectiveness, and value for money' (Crewe and Liebling, 2012b: 28). Of course, this begs the question about the views of prison officer staff, as opposed to managers. Additionally, given the differences noted earlier in relation to the quality of prison and probation services, it remains to be seen whether the same trends will be evident among probation practitioners, or, indeed, among management grades.

However, even those respondents who did not explicitly mention normative concerns about privatisation questioned the ability of the new set-up to deliver good-quality services given the problem of a fragmented and partially outsourced service. Concerns related to the quality of staff recruited, the training provided and the experience lost. There was a clear sense that probation work requires skills that need to be developed, and that it cannot be undertaken by 'just anyone'. So, even where practitioners expressed an open mind about which sector should provide probation services, their concern was with the lack of clarity of what, if any, improvement could be brought about by new governance arrangements, as well as the dangers introduced by dismantling an established existing service. Thus, the poor management of the process of transition appears to have lost any residual practitioner goodwill in relation to service provision and any support for the principles of the TR reforms. To finish off with a quote capturing a sentiment encountered frequently:

> I can't see that the shambles that looks to be unfolding will be delivering good standards of probation work any time soon.

On many levels, then, both normative and pragmatic, the introduction of TR was fundamentally at odds with the views of this sample of probation staff.

Notes

[1] See the Serious Fraud Office investigation launched in 2013 against G4S and Serco relating to overcharging of the UK government. Both companies made significant repayments to the government in 2014.

[2] For a discussion of internal and external legitimacy, see Bottoms (2003); for the lack of debate on privatisation in the prison sector, see Crewe and Liebling (2012b).

[3] In 2013/14, NOMS (2014c) rated all Probation Trusts as performing well and four Trusts as performing exceptionally well, and in 2012/13 (NOMS, 2013b), it rated five Probation Trusts as performing exceptionally well and the remainder as performing well. Merseyside Probation Trust, for example, won the 2012 UK Excellence Award by the British Quality Foundation.

5
SUBSEQUENT EVENTS – REFLECTING ON INSTITUTIONAL CHANGE AS IT HAPPENS, FURTHER DISCUSSION AND CONCLUSION

Developments since June 2014 – reflecting on institutional change as it happens

It is difficult to monitor institutional change as it happens. While the Coalition government set out its broad plans for 'Transforming Rehabilitation' (TR) early in 2013, details on the process of implementation, the problems encountered and contingency plans were difficult to locate. The public debate on the privatisation of probation was relatively muted, although it was covered systematically in the mainstream media. A sample search of *The Guardian* and *Observer* for stories discussing 'probation privatisation' between 2010 and 2015 revealed 66 items, with most items run in 2013 (26) and 2014 (20). Similarly, *The Independent* ran 34 items between 2010 and 2015. A search on the BBC website revealed coverage of the most significant events following the national probation strikes and the milestones of the TR process, with 48 items run between 2010 and 2015: 27 in 2013 and 18 in 2014. Late in 2014, a number of media programmes picked up on the 'probation crisis' in Radio BBC5Live Investigates (BBC5Live, 2014), and in January 2015, the House of Commons debated the situation in the Probation Service, with particular reference to the speed of implementation of the significant structural changes (*Hansard*, 2015).

Opponents of TR actively used social media to discuss the impact of the changes on the service and to voice their concerns. The Facebook account 'Keep Probation Public, not Private' was started in January 2013 and had 3,272 followers as of 11 February 2015. 'Jim Brown's' popular[1] 'On Probation Blog', set up in 2010, meticulously documented the implementation of TR, under the title of 'Omnishambles', and included comments by a number of probation staff. In total, 'Jim Brown' wrote 83 Omnishambles blogs and made 484 blog entries in 2014 alone.

These comments provided an impression of probation in chaos after the splitting of the service on 1 June 2014, with: inadequate information technology (IT) systems; communication problems between the National Probation Service (NPS) and the Community Rehabilitation Companies (CRCs), as well as between different NPS offices; staffing problems in the CRCs; a decline in working conditions; and an 'exodus' of experienced staff. Of course, 'evidence' from social media needs to be regarded with considerable caution. Nevertheless, it provides some insight into the world of the NPS and CRCs that would otherwise remain largely hidden.

The social media debate deserves much closer analysis than we are able to provide here. There is a significant danger in reading too much into a blog driven by dissatisfaction with, and clear opposition to, the TR agenda. Nevertheless, many of the problems identified are significant and raise real concerns over the process of implementing the controversial TR changes. These views resonate with the fears expressed by our survey respondents and further support our position that the views of our respondents are not entirely anomalous. Our survey respondents clearly objected to the principles underpinning TR, and the difficult process of transition will be unlikely to have softened those objections.

The most recent developments, as reported in the mainstream media, do not encourage hope that 2015 will bring a positive start for the new 'probation services'. Compounding these concerns, following a few months of criticism since allegations emerged in October 2014, the Chief Inspector of Probation resigned in February 2015 over a perceived conflict of interest between his role and that of his wife, who is a senior manager at Sodexo Justice Services, which secured six CRCs in the bidding process (BBC, 2015). All these developments precede one of the biggest challenges to the newly transferred CRCs. From 1 February 2015, they took on the additional responsibility of supervising offenders released from short-term prison sentences (less than 12 months). The Offender Rehabilitation Act 2014 came into force in February 2015 and social media was full of chatter at that time about the lack of probation staff training for this new legislation. The Act was introduced to respond to the high reoffending rates among short-term prisoners, many of whom have complex needs; however, there is no indication that the issues of extending statutory supervision to this group have been considered sufficiently. Concerns relate to the potential for lack of compliance among a problematic offender population and high breach rates. If such concerns come to pass, workloads in the CRCs seem bound to increase, as will court and police workloads, in response to an increase in breach proceedings.

Possible futures for probation work?

There are undoubtedly significant implications for the workforce, both practitioners and managers, within the NPS and the CRCs as a result of the TR changes themselves and of attitudes towards those changes. As argued by Bourdieu (1990), it is likely that, at this point, the future of probation work is unknowable to a significant degree and that the real outcomes of TR in terms of actual practice and the working environment and culture will not become evident for some time. Bourdieu argues that actual practice lags behind significant institutional change and that what will emerge will not be precisely that which was envisaged by the government and managers, nor practitioners.

This is because change and organisational culture and behaviour are the outcome of the complex interplay of the individuals' 'habitus' and the organisational 'field' (Bourdieu, 1977). For Bourdieu, 'habitus' constitutes the culture and working practices of individuals and small groups, while, in this context, the organisational 'field' represents the rules and expectations laid down by the government. Both the field and habitus are changed by their interaction; thus, organisational changes and practices are internalised by individuals, but they themselves change the culture and practices of the organisation. The case of TR does seem to throw these particular theories very much into the light given the speed and extent of enforced, 'top-down' institutional change involved.

One study investigating probation staff's notions of 'quality' in their work uses Bourdieu's framework. Robinson et al (2014: 126) considered that changes to probation governance and government objectives for the service (and it is noteworthy that these were pre-TR changes) constituted a significant change in the probation field that would clash with the habitus of staff. This was based on a divergence between the views of staff, on the one hand, and those of senior probation management and the government, on the other, about what was important and what constituted quality in probation work. Robinson et al found highly homogeneous views among staff about 'quality', defining it broadly in terms of: professionalism in relationships; a humanistic approach; and individual 'progress' in their supervisees. In contrast, management took a 'corporate' view of 'quality', equating it with task completion and timeliness (Robinson et al, 2014: 127–34). In overall terms, Robinson et al (2014) saw the staff habitus as being resistant to the organisational field, in ways previously reported by others (Deering, 2011; Mawby and Worrall, 2011). However, they also saw evidence of potential changes to the habitus in terms of a relative decline in practitioners considering both the social context of offending and the impact of significant others in the lives of supervisees as being of central importance to supervision. Alongside this, the case management/brokerage role was also seen as becoming potentially part of a developing habitus and supervision perhaps less of an individualised service, as practitioners reported working increasingly closely with other agencies in the overall management of offending behaviour (Robinson et al, 2014: 137).

Of course, quite how these processes will play out within TR and affect probation staff culture or habitus is yet to be discovered, but other studies have also mapped an increasing disillusion among some staff with the government's preferred direction for probation over the past decade or so (Farrow, 2004; Deering, 2011; Mawby and Worrall, 2013). Given this apparent trend and the strong views expressed by our respondents, it does seem that the implications for many within the workforce of both the CRCs and the NPS in terms of increasing disillusion and alienation and the possible resultant occupational stress do not give grounds for optimism. At the same time, these studies reported a continuing commitment of staff to the 'job', to the 'probation ideal' (if not perhaps as much to the organisation) and to providing a proper professional service to those under supervision. Some of the comments on the 'On Probation' blog also suggest as much. One commentator on the blog asked colleagues to accept that they had lost the fight to save probation and to now move on and do their jobs:

> I hope the outcome (and that's not a dirty word) for offenders and the wider community is a positive one, it's not certain right now but I know for sure it's not even likely if people don't put the things they can't change behind them and get on with the job. I'm sure this comment won't be met with a great deal of joy, but I hope that people at least consider the situation with a bit of perspective. (On Probation, 2015)

In a similar way, our respondents clearly remained committed to their work and such attitudes might mediate some of the more negatively perceived changes. Of interest also was the apparent absence of any yearning for a mythical golden age of probation, but there was clear anger at the extent of the current changes, their ideological nature and the ways in which they pose fundamental ethical and value-based, as well as clear practical, challenges to staff.

A further element to be considered is the evidence discussed earlier of some level of division between practitioners and managers, although this seems to be emerging among the former and is perhaps not evident to, or acknowledged by, the latter. Views expressed by practitioners did identify some divergence of view, with managers being seen as increasingly 'corporate' and willing to take on elements of the government's agenda, both pre-TR and around the TR changes themselves. Moreover, they were sometimes seen as becoming less interested in practice and professional issues and more so in the attainment of targets and performance management. Where there were statistically significant differences between managers and practitioners in the attitudinal data, these related to important aspects of probation practice, including the values underpinning probation work, whether probation needed to work more flexibly and support for plans to extend supervision to those serving short-term sentences (see Chapter Two).

One other 'probation tradition' that withstood previous government initiatives to change it is the continuing recruitment of individuals as practitioners who join in order to try to 'make a difference' to the lives of people under supervision, on the basis that their offending is as much to do with structural disadvantage as individual failings and that it is a collective responsibility of society to try to ameliorate such difficulties (see Farrow, 2004; Annison et al, 2008; Deering, 2010; Mawby and Worrall, 2013). As discussed in Chapter Two, in the main, our respondents joined the service for these very reasons, but it remains to be seen whether people with the same motivations will be drawn to the privatised CRCs, or, indeed, to the NPS as its position as a civil service agency may have an impact upon its attractiveness to potential recruits. Of course, as discussed earlier, the ideas of 'ownership' have a complex relationship with legitimacy in the eyes of respondents and it may be the case that the 'usual suspects' will continue to be attracted to 'the job' regardless of sector or civil service status.

Final comments and conclusion

What is clear from this research is the unequivocal opposition to the majority of the proposals within the TR document, the most fundamental of which have now come into operation. The exception seems to be the introduction of post-release supervision for short-term prisoners, but there is no doubt that TR's fundamental design and intentions were opposed in terms that revealed the feelings of anger, betrayal and sadness about the destruction of the unified, public Probation Service. It is evident that what constitutes what we have called 'probation work' was very important to respondents, but that, equally, who does it was vital: respondents had a clear antipathy to the involvement of the private sector and also, although to a lesser degree, the third sector. This was based upon a range of beliefs about governance and values. The private sector was regarded as being inevitably responsible to its shareholders and the need to make a profit, and this was seen as one of the major reasons why it would be unable to provide an appropriate service. There was clearly no agreement with government assertions that the marketisation of services would improve innovation via the discipline of competition, with this idea being regarded as ideological and without any empirical foundation. These views represent a clear rejection of the basic ideas behind the New Public Management and managerialism (see Flynn, 2002).

Respondents expressed significant pride at the achievements of the Probation Service. While the government did argue that the service 'needed' to be more innovative and that reoffending rates were 'too high' (Clarke, 2010; Ministry of Justice, 2012), these may be seen to be little more than assertions not backed up by empirical evidence. It has been argued (Deering et al, 2014) that the service was itself innovative prior to increasing levels of government control and centralisation from the early 1990s (often in a practitioner-led, 'bottom-up' fashion), although it was nowhere near as adept at carrying out thorough evaluative research on most of these practice developments (Knott, 2004). Indeed, respondents felt that the Probation Service was quite capable of innovation, but that government developments in recent decades had stifled creativity in a drive for efficiency in the pursuit of public protection and punishment.

The issue of legitimacy was also important to our respondents in terms of the public sector being seen as the only body that should be involved in the administration of punishments, however these may be envisaged. This was expressed as a matter of principle as the making of profit from punishment, and thus indirectly from crime itself, was seen as 'wrong'. However, in more pragmatic terms, privatisation was also opposed as it may place in jeopardy the professional relationship, and thus compliance, as many respondents felt that those under their supervision might be less likely to comply and otherwise cooperate with a private organisation (see McNeill and Robinson, 2013).

However, as Crewe and Liebling (2012b: 25) have suggested, legitimacy may become less of an issue pragmatically with the passage of time, but there have undoubtedly been a number of significant causes for concern about the behaviour of the private sector within criminal justice. Both G4S and Serco, who are currently involved in providing various services within criminal justice (tagging and prison contracts), were prevented by the Ministry of Justice of bidding for a CRC due to their alleged conduct under existing contracts (*The Guardian*, 2013; Howard League for Penal Reform, 2014).[2]

In addition to legitimacy and governance, respondents had a strong, normative sense of what probation work should be about. This was about engaging with individuals in a non-judgemental way, with a view to reducing their reoffending and, in this way, facilitating their rehabilitation. As part of this process, while risk assessments should be made and risk should be managed, as these were clearly fully accepted as legitimate aims, respondents were of the view that they were not sufficient. Rather, risk forms part of a wider ideal of probation work as a context and a basis for intervention aimed at rehabilitation and reducing reoffending, except in 'higher risk of harm' cases. Punishment was not mentioned, except as a small minority view, and the service was regarded as needing to provide help, in the widest sense, to individuals to address their problems, both structural and personal, with a view to rehabilitation. Although there was a bias towards the language of intervention, there was little or no mention of interventions that might be regarded, in the widest sense, as 'treatment', and what might be called 'desistance language' was in evidence with reference to 'working with people' to address problems that may be seen as blocks to desisting from crime. These broad ideas about the overall purpose of supervision can be seen in other research and back up what does seem to be a pattern of findings over the past decade (Vanstone, 2004; Canton, 2011; Deering, 2011; Mawby and Worrall, 2013).

Finally, in an attempt to answer the question we pose in the title of this report, TR clearly represents the end of the probation ideal in the sense that there is no longer a unified public sector body that carries out supervisory work with offenders subject to court orders and post-custodial licences. However, the probation ideal encompasses the wide range of tasks that we have called probation work and also a range of values and attitudes that have been outlined earlier. Many of the tasks will presumably continue, but it is far more difficult to envisage the culture and working practices within which they will take place. Perhaps some of these may experience some continuity, but it is hard to see how they will be able to flourish in the same inquisitive, contested and debated manner that has sometimes been the case within the public sector. The marketisation of part of probation has introduced a new, unwelcome dynamic to the probation field.

There is a more general question as to whether the example of the destruction of the unified Probation Service is a symptom of a wider assault on the public sector and public sector values, and a rewriting of the responsibilities and ethos of state provision in the area of criminal justice and penal policy. However, answering this question is beyond the remit of this study.

The death of probation has been announced before and, so far, semblances have always survived. Reviewing the literature on probation culture and values and listening to our survey respondents, there is some hope that probation staff, both in the NPS and the CRCs, will hold on to their values despite the new organisational and governance structure. Clare (2015: 49) suggests that probation officers in the CRCs are the 'essential carriers of the probation heritage', and given the diversity of CRC structures and ownership arrangements, there is a real potential for differing local and regional probation cultures. Additionally, the Probation Institute launched in March 2014 aims to establish itself as a centre of excellence in probation. In January 2015, it had 1,200 members and could become a repository of evidence-based practice, as well as the key values and ethics of probation work (Probation Institute, 2015). However, there is also great fear that some of the humanistic voices that were present in probation before the split will be lost. This loss is a concern not only for those encountering the Probation Service, but also for those wishing to preserve a diversity of views around criminal justice and penal policy.

Notes

[1] It is, of course, difficult to measure the reach of online blogs but the On Probation blog had 1,994332 page views as of 11 February 2015.

[2] See the Serious Fraud Office investigation launched in 2013 against G4S and Serco relating to overcharging of the UK government. Both companies made significant repayments to the government in 2014.

References

Annison, J. (2013) 'Change and the Probation Service in England and Wales: a gendered lens', *European Journal of Probation*, 5(1): 44–64.

Annison, J., Eadie, T. and Knight, C. (2008) 'People first: probation officer perspectives on probation work', *Probation Journal*, 55(3): 259–72.

Ashworth, A. and Roberts, J. (2012) 'Sentencing', in M. Maguire, R. Morgan and R. Reiner (eds) *The Oxford handbook of criminology* (5th edn), Oxford: Oxford University Press.

BBC (2013) 'Probation officers in 24-hour strike over privatisation', BBC News, 5 November. Available at: http://www.bbc.co.uk/news/uk-24814889 (accessed 11 February 2015).

BBC (2015) 'Probation chief Paul McDowell resigns over "conflict of interest"', BBC News, 2 February. Available at: http://www.bbc.co.uk/news/uk-31093568 (accessed 11 February 2015).

BBC5Live (2014) 'BBC5Live investigates', 2 November 2014. Available at: http://www.bbc.co.uk/podcasts/series/5linvestigates/all (accessed 11 February 2015).

Bottoms, A. (2003) 'Theoretical reflections on the evaluation of a penal policy initiative', in L. Zedner and A. Ashworth (eds) *The criminological foundations of penal policy*, Oxford: Oxford University Press.

Bottoms, A. and McWilliams, W. (1979) 'A non-treatment paradigm for probation practice', *British Journal of Social Work*, 9: 159–202.

Bourdieu, P. (1977) *Outline of a theory of practice*, Cambridge: Cambridge University Press.

Bourdieu, P. (1990) *The logic of practice*, Cambridge: Polity Press.

Brown, J., Cooper, G. and Kirkcaldy, B. (1996) 'Occupational stress among senior police officers', *British Journal of Psychology*, 87(1): 31–41.

Burke, L. (2013) 'Editorial: Grayling's hubris', *Probation Journal*, 60(4): 377–82.

Burke, L. and Collett, S. (2010) 'People are not things: what New Labour has done to probation', *Probation Journal*, 57(3): 232–49.

Burke, L. and Davies, K. (2011) 'Editorial: introducing the special edition on occupational culture and skills in probation practice', *European Journal of Probation*, 3(1): 1–13.

Burnett, R. and McNeill, F. (2005) 'The place of the officer–offender relationship in assisting offenders to desist from crime', *Probation Journal*, 52(3): 247–68.

Canton, R. (2011) *Probation: working with offenders*, London: Routledge.

Carter, P. (2003) *Managing offenders, reducing crime: the correctional services review*, London: Home Office Strategy Unit.

Cheliotis, L.K. (2006) 'How iron is the iron cage of new penology? The role of human agency in the implementation of criminal justice policy', *Punishment and Society*, 8(3): 313–40.

Clare, R. (2015) 'Maintaining professional practice: the role of the probation officer in community rehabilitation companies', *Probation Journal*, 62(1): 49–61.

Clarke, K. (2010) 'Last update, revolving door of crime and reoffending to stop says Clarke'. Available at: http://www.cjp.org.uk/news/archive/revolving-door-of-crime-and-reoffending-to-stop-says-clarke-30-06-2010/ (accessed 28 July 2010).

Collett, S. (2013) 'Riots, revolution and rehabilitation: the future of probation', *Howard Journal of Criminal Justice*, 52(2): 163–89.

Crewe, B. and Liebling, A. (2012a) 'Liberal-humanitarian penal values and practices', in T. Ugelvik and J. Dullum (eds) *Penal exceptionalism? Nordic prison policy and practice*, London: Routledge.

Crewe, B. and Liebling, A. (2012b) 'Insider views of private sector competition', in V. Helyar-Cardwell (ed) *Delivering justice: the role of the public, private and voluntary sectors in the prison system*, London: Criminal Justice Alliance Publications.

Crook, R. and Wood, D. (2014) 'The customer is always right'? Consumerism and the Probation Service', *European Journal of Probation*, 6(1): 57–66.

Deering, J. (2010) 'Attitudes and beliefs of trainee probation officers – a new breed?', *Probation Journal*, 57(1): 9–26.

Deering, J. (2011) *Probation practice and the new penology: practitioner reflections*, Aldershot: Ashgate.

Deering, J., Feilzer, M. and Holmes, T. (2014) 'The transition from public to private in probation – values and attitudes of managers in the private sector', *Probation Journal*, 61(3): 234–50.

Farrall, S. (2002) *Rethinking what works with offenders*, Cullompton: Willan.

Farrow, K. (2004) 'Still committed after all these years? Morale in the modern-day Probation Service', *Probation Journal*, 51(3): 206–20.

Feeley, M. and Simon, J. (1992) 'The new penology: notes on the emerging strategy for corrections', *Criminology*, 30(4): 449–75.

Feilzer, M.Y. and Trew, J. (2012) 'The impact of value based decision making on policing in North Wales. Final report to the Welsh Government'. Available at: http://wales.gov.uk/docs/caecd/research/130122-Impact-Value-Based-Decision-Making-Policing-North-Wales-En.Pdf (accessed 28 November 2014).

Fitzgibbon, W. and Lea, J. (2014) 'Defending probation: beyond privatisation and security', *European Journal of Probation*, 6(1): 24–41.

Flynn, N. (2002) 'Organisation and management: a changing agenda', in D. Ward, J. Scott and M. Lacey (eds) *Probation: working for justice* (2nd edn), Oxford: Oxford University Press.

Garland, D. (2001) *The culture of control*, Oxford: Oxford University Press.

Genders, E. (2002) 'Legitimacy, accountability and private prisons', *Punishment and Society*, 4(3): 285–303.

Hansard (2011) House of Commons, 9 November, col 393w,.

Hansard (2015) 'House of Commons: Probation Service debate', 13 January. Available at: http://www.publications.parliament.uk/pa/cm201415/cmhansrd/cm150113/halltext/150113h0002.htm (accessed 11 February 2015).

HMIP (2014) 'Transforming Rehabilitation: early implementation'. Available at: http://www.justiceinspectorates.gov.uk/hmiprobation/inspections/trearlyimplementation/#.VRP-cZisVyg (accessed 11 February 2015).

Home Office (1984) *Statement of national objectives and priorities*, London: Home Office.

Home Office (1992) *National Standards for the supervision of offenders in the community*, London: Home Office.

Home Office (1995) *Strengthening punishment in the community*, London: HMSO.

Home Office (1996) *Protecting the public*, London: HMSO.

Home Office (1998) *Effective Practice Initiative: probation circular 35/98*, London: Home Office.

Home Office (2000) *National Standards for the supervision of offenders in the community*, London: Home Office.

Home Office (2001) *A new choreography. An integrated strategy for the National Probation Service for England and Wales*, London: Home Office.

Hough, M., Jackson, J., Bradford, B., Myhill, A. and Quinton, P. (2010) 'Procedural justice, trust and institutional legitimacy', *Policing: A Journal of Policy and Practice*, 4(3): 203–10.

Howard League for Penal Reform (2014) *Corporate crime? A dossier of the failure of privatisation in the criminal justice system*, London: The Howard League for Penal Reform.

Hucklesby, A. (2013) 'Compliance with electronically monitored curfew orders: some empirical findings', in A. Crawford and A. Hucklesby (eds) *Legitimacy and compliance in criminal justice*, Abingdon: Routledge.

Jackson, J., Tyler, T.R., Bradford, B., Taylor, D. and Shiner, M. (2010) 'Legitimacy and procedural justice in prisons', *Prison Service Journal*, 191: 4–10.

Kemshall, H. (2003) *Understanding risk in criminal justice*, Maidenhead: Open University Press.

King, S. (2013) 'Assisted desistance and experiences of probation supervision', *Probation Journal*, 60(2): 136–51.

Kinman, G., Clements, A. and Hart, J. (2014) 'POA members' stress and work-related wellbeing survey'. Available at: http://www.workstress. net/downloads/poa%20survey.pdf (accessed 9 January 2015).

Knott, C. (2004) 'Evidence-based practice in the National Probation Service', in R. Burnett and C. Roberts (eds) *What works in probation and youth justice: developing evidence-based practice*, Cullompton: Willan

Leftly, M. (2014a) 'Probation Service in chaos as systems wipe offenders' data', *Independent*, 22 June. Available at: http://www. independent.co.uk/news/uk/home-news/probation-service-in-chaos-as-systems-wipe-offenders-data-9554444.html (accessed 22 June 2014).

Leftly, M. (2014b) 'Probation bidders may make a profit, but they'll never be popular', *Independent*, 5 September. Available at: http:// www.Independent.Co.Uk/News/Business/Comment/Mark-Leftly-Probation-Bidders-May-Make-A-Profit-But-Theyll-Never-Be-Popular-9713354.html (accessed 5 September 2014).

Leftly, M. (2014c) 'Fury over £15m bill for consultant on probation deal', *Independent*, 13 November. Available at: http://www. independent.co.uk/news/business/news/fury-over-15m-bill-for-consultants-on-probation-deal-9859922.html (accessed 16 November 2014).

Lezard, T. (2014) 'Poll: 99% of probation officers oppose government reforms', 3 September. Available at: http://Union-News. Co.Uk/2014/09/Poll-99-Probation-Officers-Oppose-Government-Reforms/?Doing_Wp_Cron=1410269590.828526 0200500488281250 (accessed 3 September 2014).

Liebling, A. (2004) *Prisons and their moral performance: a study of values, quality, and prison life*, Oxford: Clarendon Press.

Lipton, D., Martinson, R. and Wilks, J. (1975) *The effectiveness of correctional treatment*, New York, NY: Praeger.

Maguire, M. and Raynor, P. (2010) 'Putting the OM into NOMS: problems and possibilities for offender management', in J. Brayford, F. Cowe and J. Deering (eds) *What else works? Creative work with offenders*, Cullompton: Willan.

Mawby, R.C. and Worrall, A. (2011) 'Probation workers and their occupational cultures', Final Report to the EESRC. Available at: http://www2.le.ac.uk/departments/criminology/research/current-projects/rim3_culture_probation (accessed 11 February 2015).

Mawby, R.C. and Worrall, A. (2013) *Doing probation work: identity in a criminal justice occupation*, Abingdon: Routledge.

McGuire, J. (2001) 'What works in correctional intervention? Evidence and practical implications', in G. Bernfeld, D. Farrington and A. Leschied (eds) *Offender rehabilitation in practice: implementing and evaluating effective programs*, Chichester: Wiley.

McNeill, F. and Robinson, G. (2013) 'Liquid legitimacy and community sanctions', in A. Crawford and A. Hucklesby (eds) *Legitimacy and compliance in criminal justice*, Abingdon: Routledge.

Ministry of Justice (2011) *Competition strategy for offender services*, London: Ministry of Justice.

Ministry of Justice (2012) *Punishment and reform. Effective community sentences*, Consultation Paper CP8/2012, London: Ministry of Justice.

Ministry of Justice (2013) *Transforming Rehabilitation: a strategy for reform*, May, London: Ministry of Justice.

Ministry of Justice (2014a) 'Workforce information summary report, Q4 2013/14'. Available at: https://www.gov.uk/government/statistics/probation-service-quarterly-reports-20132014 (accessed 4 November 2014).

Ministry of Justice (2014b) *2011 PBR payment mechanism baselines and thresholds by CPA*, October, London: Ministry of Justice.

Ministry of Justice (2014c) 'The Transforming Rehabilitation programme: the new owners of the CRCs'. Available at: https://www.gov.uk/government/policies/reducing-reoffending-and-improving-rehabilitation/supporting-pages/transforming-rehabilitation (accessed 26 January 2015).

Napo (2006) *Probation values: commitment to best practice*, London: Napo.

Napo (2007) *Changing lives: an oral history of probation*, London: Napo.

Napo (2010) 'Only 24% direct contact time – it's official!', *Napo News*, January.

Napo (2013) 'Justice not for sale: time for action!', *Napo News*, May.

Napo (2014) 'Probation privatisation: huge business risks', *Napo News*, March.

Napo (2015) 'The impact of "Transforming Rehabilitation" on the Probation Service', Napo briefing for Parliamentarians, January. Available at: https://www.napo.org.uk/campaigning (accessed 11 February 2015).

Nellis, M. (1999) 'Towards the field of corrections: modernising the Probation Service in the late 1990s', *Social Policy*, 33(3): 302–23.

Nellis, M. and Gelsthorpe, L. (2003) 'Human rights and the probation values debate', in W. Chui and M. Nellis (eds) *Moving probation forward*, Harlow: Pearson.

Newburn, T. (2003) *Crime and criminal justice policy* (2nd edn), Harlow: Longman.

NNC (National Negotiating Council) (2014) 'The National Negotiating Council for the Probation Service: National Agreement on pay and conditions of service'. Available at: http://www.probationassociation.co.uk/media/3190/nnc-agreement-on-pay-and-conditions-21-May-2014.Pdf (accessed 13 January 2015).

NOMS (National Offender Management Service) (2013a) *Offender Engagement Programme news – final edition*, March, London: NOMS.

NOMS (2013b) 'Probation Trusts' annual performance rating, 2012/13'. Available at: https://www.gov.uk/government/statistics/prison-and-probation-trusts-performance-statistics-201213 (accessed 11 February 2015).

NOMS (2014a) 'Case allocation', PI 05/2014. Available at: https://www.justice.gov.uk/offenders/probation-instructions (accessed 20 January 2015).

NOMS (2014b) 'Process for community rehabilitation companies to refer cases in custody or the community to the National Probation Service for risk review, including escalation', PI 57/2014. Available at: https://www.justice.gov.uk/downloads/offenders/psipso/psi-2014/psi-41-2014-Pi-57-2014-Risk-Escalation.Pdf (accessed 20 January 2015).

NOMS (2014c) '"Probation Trusts" annual performance rating, 2013/14'. Available at: https://www.gov.uk/government/uploads/system/uploads/attachment_data/file/338962/probation-trust-perf-ratings-2013-14.Pdf (accessed 11 February 2015).

On Probation (2015) 'Pleasing everyone', blog, 9 February. Available at: http://probationmatters.blogspot.co.uk/2015/02/pleasing-everyone.html (accessed 11 February 2015).

Parliamentary Select Committee on Public Administration (2002) 'Seventh report on public administration', 24 June. Available at: http://www.publications.parliament.uk/pa/cm200102/cmselect/cmpubadm/263/26304.htm (accessed 24 May 2013).

Politics.co.uk (2014) 'Chaos in probation: staff "picked out of a hat" for privatised service', 3 July. Available at: http://www.politics.co.uk/news/2014/07/03/chaos-in-probation-staff-picked-out-of-a-hat-for-privatised (accessed 9 January 2015).

Probation Institute (2015) 'First reflections: 1,200 members'. Available at: http://probation-institute.org/first-post/ (accessed 15 January 2015).

Raynor, P. (2004) 'Rehabilitative and reintegrative approaches', in A. Bottoms, S. Rex and G. Robinson (eds) *Alternatives to prison: Options for an insecure society*, Cullompton: Willan.

Raynor, P. (2012) 'Community penalties, probation and offender management', in M. Maguire, R. Morgan and R. Reiner (eds) *The Oxford handbook of criminology* (5th edn), Oxford: Oxford University Press.

Raynor, P. and Maguire, M. (2006) 'End-to-end or end in tears? Prospects for the effectiveness of the national offender management model', in M. Hough, R. Allen and U. Padel (eds) *Reshaping probation and prisons: the new offender management framework*, Bristol: The Policy Press.

Raynor, P. and Vanstone, M. (2002) *Understanding community penalties: probation, policy and social change*, Buckingham: Open University Press.

Raynor, P., Ugwudike, P. and Vanstone, M. (2013) 'The impact of skills in probation work: a reconviction study', *Criminology and Criminal Justice*, 14(2): 235–49.

Rex, S. (1999) 'Desistance from offending: experiences of probation', *Howard Journal of Criminal Justice*, 38(4): 366–383.

Robinson, G. (2008) 'Late-modern rehabilitation: the evolution of a penal strategy', *Punishment and Society*, 10(4): 429–45.

Robinson, G. and Burnett, R. (2007) 'Experiencing modernisation: frontline probation perspectives on the transition to a national offender management service', *Probation Journal*, 54(4): 318–37.

Robinson, G. and McNeill, F. (2004) 'Purposes matter: examining the "ends" of probation', in G. Mair (ed) *What matters in probation*, Cullompton: Willan.

Robinson, G., Priede, C., Farrall, S., Shapland, J. and McNeill, F. (2014) 'Understanding "quality" in probation practice: frontline perspectives in England and Wales', *Criminology and Criminal Justice*, 14(2): 123–42.

Schonlau, M., Van Soest, A., Kapteyn, A. and Couper, M. (2009) 'Selection bias in Web surveys and the use of propensity scores', *Sociological Methods and Research*, 37(3): 291–318.

Straw, J. (1997) *Commons written reply*, Hansard, London: Houses of Parliament.

Straw, J. (2007) *Letter to Neil Gerrard, M.P.*, London: Ministry of Justice.

Sunshine, J. and Tyler, T. (2003) 'The role of procedural justice and legitimacy in shaping public support for policing', *Law and Society Review*, 37(3): 513–48.

The Guardian (2013) 'G4S and Serco stripped of offender tagging contracts over fraud claims'. Available: http://www.theguardian.com/uk-news/2013/dec/12/g4s-serco-tagging-contracts-fraud-allegations-monitoring-criminals (accessed 12 December 2013).

Tyler, T. (2006) *Why people obey the law*, New Jersey, NJ: Princeton University Press.

Vanstone, M. (2004) *Supervising offenders in the community: a history of probation theory and practice*, Aldershot: Ashgate.

Weaver, B. and McNeill, F. (2010) 'Travelling hopefully: desistance theory and probation practice', in J. Brayford, F. Cowe and J. Deering (eds) *What else works? Creative work with offenders*, Cullompton: Willan.

Williams, B. (1995) *Probation value*, London: Venture Press.

Zedner, L. (2002) 'Danger of dystopias in penal theory', *Oxford Journal of Legal Studies*, 22(2): 341–66.

APPENDICES

Appendix 1: Full tables of survey attitudinal data

The government is right to claim that in order to make rehabilitation more flexible and creative, it needs to be opened up to market competition.

	Frequency	Percent	Valid Percent
Strongly Agree	8	.6	1.0
Agree	19	1.4	2.4
Neither Agree nor Disagree	30	2.3	3.7
Disagree	137	10.5	17.0
Strongly Disagree	612	46.7	75.9
Total	**806**	**61.5**	**100.0**
Missing	505	38.5	
Total	1311	100.0	

Individuals I supervise have expressed concerns about being supervised by a private or third sector organisation in the future.

	Frequency	Percent	Valid Percent
Strongly Agree	367	28.0	46.0
Agree	239	18.2	29.9
Neither Agree nor Disagree	148	11.3	18.5
Disagree	25	1.9	3.1
Strongly Disagree	19	1.4	2.4
Total	**798**	**60.9**	**100.0**
Missing	513	39.1	
Total	1311	100.0	

The government's ideas for change contained within *Transforming Rehabilitation* are not based on any evidence of the greater effectiveness of the private or third sectors in working with offenders.

	Frequency	Percent	Valid Percent
Strongly Agree	680	51.9	85.0
Agree	91	6.9	11.4
Neither Agree nor Disagree	15	1.1	1.9
Disagree	3	.2	.4
Strongly Disagree	11	.8	1.4
Total	**800**	**61.0**	**100.0**
Missing	511	39.0	
Total	1311	100.0	

The Probation Service is unique because of the values underpinning its work.

	Frequency	Percent	Valid Percent
Strongly Agree	533	40.7	67.0
Agree	178	13.6	22.4
Neither Agree nor Disagree	62	4.7	7.8
Disagree	15	1.1	1.9
Strongly Disagree	7	.5	.9
Total	**795**	**60.6**	**100.0**
Missing	516	39.4	
Total	1311	100.0	

The existing Probation Service would be able to deliver more flexible and creative rehabilitation services if the government allowed it to do so.

	Frequency	Percent	Valid Percent
Strongly Agree	670	51.1	84.7
Agree	95	7.2	12.0
Neither Agree nor Disagree	16	1.2	2.0
Disagree	3	.2	.4
Strongly Disagree	7	.5	.9
Total	**791**	**60.3**	**100.0**
Missing	520	39.7	
Total	1311	100.0	

It is important in terms of compliance that individual offenders see the organisation supervising them as legitimate.

	Frequency	Percent	Valid Percent
Strongly Agree	678	51.7	85.3
Agree	106	8.1	13.3
Neither Agree nor Disagree	10	.8	1.3
Disagree	1	.1	.1
Total	**795**	**60.6**	**100.0**
Missing	516	39.4	
Total	1311	100.0	

Payment by Results is a good idea because it will provide necessary incentives for individuals to do a good job.

	Frequency	Percent	Valid Percent
Strongly Agree	7	.5	.9
Agree	13	1.0	1.6
Neither Agree nor Disagree	46	3.5	5.8
Disagree	165	12.6	20.8
Strongly Disagree	562	42.9	70.9
Total	**793**	60.5	100.0
Missing	518	39.5	
Total	1311	100.0	

The Probation Service is bureaucratic and inflexible and unable to deliver more flexible supervision.

	Frequency	Percent	Valid Percent
Strongly Agree	41	3.1	5.2
Agree	110	8.4	13.9
Neither Agree nor Disagree	113	8.6	14.2
Disagree	295	22.5	37.2
Strongly Disagree	234	17.8	29.5
Total	**793**	**60.5**	**100.0**
Missing	518	39.5	
Total	1311	100.0	

I am worried about my own future in terms of the stability of my employment if I transfer to a private or third sector organisation.

	Frequency	Percent	Valid Percent
Strongly Agree	558	42.6	69.8
Agree	166	12.7	20.8
Neither Agree nor Disagree	52	4.0	6.5
Disagree	15	1.1	1.9
Strongly Disagree	8	.6	1.0
Total	**799**	**60.9**	**100.0**
Missing	512	39.1	
Total	1311	100.0	

Working for a Community Rehabilitation Company (CRC) will limit my professional development due to only working with 'lower-risk' offenders

	Frequency	Percent	Valid Percent
Strongly Agree	486	37.1	61.1
Agree	163	12.4	20.5
Neither Agree nor Disagree	102	7.8	12.8
Disagree	35	2.7	4.4
Strongly Disagree	9	.7	1.1
Total	**795**	**60.6**	**100.0**
Missing	516	39.4	
Total	1311	100.0	

The attitude of private and third sector companies towards compliance and enforcement will not be influenced by Payment by Results.

	Frequency	Percent	Valid Percent
Strongly Agree	73	5.6	9.2
Agree	31	2.4	3.9
Neither Agree nor Disagree	38	2.9	4.8
Disagree	133	10.1	16.8
Strongly Disagree	517	39.4	65.3
Total	**792**	**60.4**	**100.0**
Missing	519	39.6	
Total	1311	100.0	

I am considering looking for another job because of my concerns about my own future and the future of the Probation Service.

	Frequency	Percent	Valid Percent
Strongly Agree	358	27.3	44.9
Agree	247	18.8	31.0
Neither Agree nor Disagree	123	9.4	15.4
Disagree	56	4.3	7.0
Strongly Disagree	13	1.0	1.6
Total	797	60.8	100.0
Missing	514	39.2	
Total	1311	100.0	

Punishment (including community sentences and licences) should only be delivered by agencies of the state.

	Frequency	Percent	Valid Percent
Strongly Agree	611	46.6	76.9
Agree	118	9.0	14.8
Neither Agree nor Disagree	43	3.3	5.4
Disagree	19	1.4	2.4
Strongly Disagree	4	.3	.5
Total	**795**	**60.6**	**100.0**
Missing	516	39.4	
Total	1311	100.0	

Offenders are less likely to comply with orders if they are supervised by private and/or third sector organisations.

	Frequency	Percent	Valid Percent
Strongly Agree	277	21.1	34.8
Agree	274	20.9	34.5
Neither Agree nor Disagree	196	15.0	24.7
Disagree	38	2.9	4.8
Strongly Disagree	10	.8	1.3
Total	**795**	**60.6**	**100.0**
Missing	516	39.4	
Total	1311	100.0	

It does not matter who delivers community orders as long as the service is of a good quality.

	Frequency	Percent	Valid Percent
Strongly Agree	18	1.4	2.3
Agree	84	6.4	10.6
Neither Agree nor Disagree	94	7.2	11.8
Disagree	252	19.2	31.7
Strongly Disagree	346	26.4	43.6
Total	**794**	**60.6**	**100.0**
Missing	517	39.4	
Total	1311	100.0	

Private sector companies will see the provision of a quality service as the best way to make a profit.

	Frequency	Percent	Valid Percent
Strongly Agree	98	7.5	12.4
Agree	74	5.6	9.4
Neither Agree nor Disagree	62	4.7	7.9
Disagree	206	15.7	26.1
Strongly Disagree	348	26.5	44.2
Total	**788**	**60.1**	**100.0**
Missing	523	39.9	
Total	1311	100.0	

Private and third sector organisations can react more quickly to changing circumstances and be more flexible than the Probation Service.

	Frequency	Percent	Valid Percent
Strongly Agree	13	1.0	1.6
Agree	62	4.7	7.8
Neither Agree nor Disagree	116	8.8	14.6
Disagree	238	18.2	30.0
Strongly Disagree	365	27.8	46.0
Total	794	**60.6**	**100.0**
Missing	517	39.4	
Total	1311	100.0	

Working for the private sector will open up more career opportunities for me.

	Frequency	Percent	Valid Percent
Strongly Agree	4	.3	.5
Agree	39	3.0	4.9
Neither Agree nor Disagree	235	17.9	29.7
Disagree	201	15.3	25.4
Strongly Disagree	313	23.9	39.5
Total	**792**	**60.4**	**100.0**
Missing	519	39.6	
Total	1311	100.0	

The government is pursuing these changes as a result of an ideological commitment to reducing the size of the state.

	Frequency	Percent	Valid Percent
Strongly Agree	525	40.0	66.7
Agree	120	9.2	15.2
Neither Agree nor Disagree	105	8.0	13.3
Disagree	20	1.5	2.5
Strongly Disagree	17	1.3	2.2
Total	787	60.0	100.0
Missing	524	40.0	
Total	1311	100.0	

The new National Probation Service (NPS) is a good idea as it will provide a real opportunity to specialise in working with higher-risk individuals and protecting the public.

	Frequency	Percent	Valid Percent
Strongly Agree	10	.8	1.3
Agree	34	2.6	4.3
Neither Agree nor Disagree	123	9.4	15.4
Disagree	250	19.1	31.3
Strongly Disagree	382	29.1	47.8
Total	**799**	**60.9**	**100.0**
Missing	512	39.1	
Total	1311	100.0	

There are bound to be problems of communication between the CRCs and the NPS that will cause problems in individual cases.

	Frequency	Percent	Valid Percent
Strongly Agree	679	51.8	84.6
Agree	99	7.6	12.3
Neither Agree nor Disagree	14	1.1	1.7
Disagree	3	.2	.4
Strongly Disagree	8	.6	1.0
Total	**803**	**61.3**	**100.0**
Missing	508	38.7	
Total	1311	100.0	

Appendix 2: Respondent demographics

Are you?

	Frequency	Percent	Valid Percent
Female	777	59.3	64.9
Male	421	32.1	35.1
Total	**1198**	**91.4**	**100.0**
Missing	113	8.6	
Total	1311	100.0	

What is your current grade?

	Frequency	Percent	Valid Percent
Case Administrator	38	2.9	3.2
PSO	270	20.6	22.7
PO	628	47.9	52.8
Team Manager	155	11.8	13.0
Grade Above Team Manager	26	2.0	2.2
Other	72	5.5	6.1
Total	**1189**	**90.7**	**100.0**
Missing	122	9.3	
Total	1311	100.0	

Note: PSO - Probation Service Officer; PO - Probation Officer

What professional qualification do you have?

	Frequency	Percent	Valid Percent
PQF VQ Level 3	139	10.6	11.8
PQF BA	139	10.6	11.8
DiPS	364	27.8	30.9
DipSW	99	7.6	8.4
CQSW	174	13.3	14.8
Not qualified	119	9.1	10.1
Other	144	11.0	12.2
Total	**1178**	**89.9**	**100.0**
Missing	133	10.1	
Total	1311	100.0	

Note: PQF VQ Level 3 - Probation Qualification Framework Vocational Qualification; PQF BA - Probation Qualification Framework Bachelor of Arts; DiPS - Diploma n Probation Studies; DipSW - Diploma in Social Work; CQSW - Certificate of Qualification in Social Work

How long have you worked for the Probation Service?

	Frequency	Percent	Valid Percent
0–3 years	48	3.7	4.0
4–6 years	102	7.8	8.5
7–9 years	245	18.7	20.5
10+ years	801	61.1	67.0
Total	**1196**	**91.2**	**100.0**
Missing	115	8.8	
Total	1311	100.0	

Appendix 3: The full survey

Probation Workers' Views on 'Transforming Rehabilitation'

1. Introduction

This questionnaire seeks to explore the views of probation workers about government intentions to marketise and part-privatise the service's functions, as outlined in Transforming Rehabilitation . This proposed the creation of 'Community Rehabilitation Companies' (CRCs) which will in due course be subject to marketisation and privatisation and a new National Probation Service, which will be part of the civil service.

We are interested in the views of probation workers about these proposals and would be grateful if you would complete the following questionnaire. There are both open and closed questions. For the former, there are 'text boxes' that should give sufficient room for you to write as much as you would like.

The questionnaire is anonymous - you are not asked for any personal details that would enable you to be identified, only some basic demographic information.

The questionnaire should not take you more than 20 minutes to complete. PLEASE NOTE: you are able to save your responses and return to the questionnaire later. However, to do this you must use the same computer and web browser each time you access the questionnaire. This is also dependent upon certain cookies being enabled on your computer, so we would advise completing it in one go. The questionnaire is open until 30th April 2014.

By completing the questionnaire, we will regard you as having given informed consent to participate. The results will be analysed with a view to publishing in an academic journal.

PLEASE NOTE: you may receive this questionnaire via Napo or your Probation Trust. Please complete it only once.

If you have any queries about the research, please feel free to contact either of us by email at: m.feilzer@bangor.ac.uk or john.deering@southwales.ac.uk

Thanks in anticipation,
Martina Feilzer, Bangor University
John Deering, University of South Wales

1. How did you receive this questionnaire?

○ Via Napo

○ Via Probation Trust

Probation Workers' Views on 'Transforming Rehabilitation'

2. Your details

1. Are you?

○ Female

○ Male

2. What is your current grade? (indicate one)

○ Case Administrator

○ PSC

○ PO

○ Team Manager

○ Grade Above Team Manager

○ Other

Other (please specify)

[   ]

3. What professional qualification do you have? (indicate one)

○ PQF VQ Level 3

○ PQF BA

○ DiPS

○ DipSW

○ CQSW

○ Not qualified

○ Other

Other (please specify)

[   ]

4. How long have you worked for the probation service? (indicate one)

○ 0-3 years

○ 4-6 years

○ 7-9 years

○ 10+ years

5. Please indicate which probation trust you are working for:

[   ]

Probation Workers' Views on 'Transforming Rehabilitation'

6. Please describe briefly your current job role, in terms of tasks and level of risk :

Probation Workers' Views on 'Transforming Rehabilitation'

3. Joining and working in the probation service

1. What were your reasons for joining the probation service?

2. Has working for the service lived up to your expectations?

○ Yes

○ No

○ Partly

Please give reasons

3. What do you think should be the job of the probation service?

APPENDICES

4. Do you think that the probation service is underpinned by an agreed set of values? (indicate one)

◯ Yes

◯ No

◯ Don't Know

Please give reasons. If you answered 'yes', what are those values?

133

Probation Workers' Views on 'Transforming Rehabilitation'

4. Transforming Rehabilitation

1. Do you think that the government is right to try to address re-offending by short-term (up to 12 months) ex-prisoners by making them subject to supervision on release? (indicate one)

○ Yes

○ No

○ Undecided

2. Who might be best placed to undertake this work? (indicate one).

○ The existing probation service

○ The private sector

○ The third sector

Please give reasons

3. Do you think the government is right in thinking that offender supervision needs to become more 'flexible and creative'? (indicate one)

○ Yes

○ No

○ Undecided

Please give reasons

Probation Workers' Views on 'Transforming Rehabilitation'

4. Who might be best placed to undertake this work? (indicate one).

○ The existing probation service

○ The private sector

○ The third sector

Please give reasons

Probation Workers' Views on 'Transforming Rehabilitation'

5. Working for the third or private sectors

1. Do you think working for the private sector would be : better/worse/no different than working for the probation service? (indicate one)

◯ Better

◯ Worse

◯ No different

Please give reasons

2. Do you think working for the third sector would be: better/worse/no different than working for the probation service? (indicate one)

◯ Better

◯ Worse

◯ No different

Please give reasons

3. What do you think the private sector has to offer to the provision of services for individuals on supervision?

Probation Workers' Views on 'Transforming Rehabilitation'

4. What do you think the third sector has to offer to the provision of services for individuals on supervision?

5. What do you think the private sector has to offer to the carrying out of risk assessments and the protection of the public?

6. What do you think the third sector has to offer to the carrying out of risk assessments and the protection of the public?

Probation Workers' Views on 'Transforming Rehabilitation'

6. Working for the new National Probation Service

**1. Do you think working for the new National Probation Service would be:
better/worse/no different from working in the existing probation service (indicate one)**

◯ Better

◯ Worse

◯ No Different

Please give reasons

2. What issues might be important in the relationship between the National Probation Service and the Community Rehabilitation Companies?

Probation Workers' Views on 'Transforming Rehabilitation'

7. Miscellaneous

1. If you were starting with a blank sheet, how would you organise community supervision in terms of a public/private/third sector balance?

2. What might be the impact of Payment by Results on the provision of community supervision?

3. Does it matter who does 'probation work' as long as it is done well? (indicate one)

○ Yes
○ No
○ Undecided

Please give reasons

Probation Workers' Views on 'Transforming Rehabilitation'

4. Assuming all of the following to be possible, what would be your preferred option in terms of your future employment? (indicate one)

○ Continue to work for the existing probation service

○ Work for a CRC for a private sector company

○ Work for a CRC for a third sector organisation

○ Work for the new NPS

Please give reasons

Probation Workers' Views on 'Transforming Rehabilitation'

8. Please indicate your level of agreement/disagreement with the following sta...

Please indicate one response to each statement

1. The Government is right to claim that in order to make rehabilitation more flexible and creative, it needs to be opened up to market competition.

Strongly Agree	Agree	Neither Agree nor Disagree	Disagree	Strongly Disagree
○	○	○	○	○

2. Individuals I supervise have expressed concerns about being supervised by a private or third sector organisation in the future.

Strongly Agree	Agree	Neither Agree nor Disagree	Disagree	Strongly Disagree
○	○	○	○	○

3. The Government's ideas for change contained within Transforming Rehabilitation are not based on any evidence of the greater effectiveness of the private or third sectors in working with offenders.

Strongly Agree	Agree	Neither Agree nor Disagree	Disagree	Strongly Disagree
○	○	○	○	○

4. The probation service is unique because of the values underpinning its work.

Strongly Agree	Agree	Neither Agree nor Disagree	Disagree	Strongly Disagree
○	○	○	○	○

5. The existing probation service would be able to deliver more flexible and creative rehabilitation services if the government allowed it to do so.

Strongly Agree	Agree	Neither Agree nor Disagree	Disagree	Strongly Disagree
○	○	○	○	○

6. It is important in terms of compliance that individuals on supervision see the organisation supervising them as legitimate.

Strongly Agree	Agree	Neither Agree nor Disagree	Disagree	Strongly Disagree
○	○	○	○	○

7. Payment by Results is a good idea because it will provide necessary incentives for individuals to do a good job.

Strongly Agree	Agree	Neither Agree nor Disagree	Disagree	Strongly Disagree
○	○	○	○	○

8. The probation service is bureaucratic and inflexible and unable to deliver more flexible supervision.

Strongly Agree	Agree	Neither Agree nor Disagree	Disagree	Strongly Disagree
○	○	○	○	○

Page 13

Probation Workers' Views on 'Transforming Rehabilitation'

9. I am worried about my own future in terms of the stability of my employment if I transfer to a private or third sector organisation.

Strongly Agree	Agree	Neither Agree nor Disagree	Disagree	Strongly Disagree
○	○	○	○	○

10. Working for a CRC will limit my professional development due to only working with 'lower risk' individuals.

Strongly Agree	Agree	Neither Agree nor Disagree	Disagree	Strongly Disagree
○	○	○	○	○

11. The attitude of private and third sector organisations towards compliance and enforcement will not be influenced because of Payment by Results.

Strongly Agree	Agree	Neither Agree nor Disagree	Disagree	Strongly Disagree
○	○	○	○	○

12. I am considering looking for another job because of my concerns about my own future and the future of the probation service.

Strongly Agree	Agree	Neither Agree nor Disagree	Disagree	Strongly Disagree
○	○	○	○	○

13. Punishment (including community sentences and licences) should only be delivered by agencies of the state.

Strongly Agree	Agree	Neither Agree nor Disagree	Disagree	Strongly Disagree
○	○	○	○	○

14. Offenders are less likely to comply with orders if they are supervised by private and/or third sector organisations.

Strongly Agree	Agree	Neither Agree nor Disagree	Disagree	Strongly Disagree
○	○	○	○	○

15. It does not matter who delivers community orders as long as the service is of a good quality.

Strongly Agree	Agree	Neither Agree nor Disagree	Disagree	Strongly Disagree
○	○	○	○	○

16. Private sector companies will see the provision of a quality service as the best way to make a profit.

Strongly Agree	Agree	Neither Agree nor Disagree	Disagree	Strongly Disagree
○	○	○	○	○

17. Private and third sector organisations can react more quickly to changing circumstances and be more flexible than the probation service.

Strongly Agree	Agree	Neither Agree nor Disagree	Disagree	Strongly Disagree
○	○	○	○	○

Probation Workers' Views on 'Transforming Rehabilitation'

18. Working for the private sector will open up more career opportunities for me.

Strongly Agree	Agree	Neither Agree nor Disagree	Disagree	Strongly Disagree
○	○	○	○	○

19. The Government is pursuing these changes as a result of an ideological commitment to reducing the size of the state.

Strongly Agree	Agree	Neither Agree nor Disagree	Disagree	Strongly Disagree
○	○	○	○	○

20. The new NPS is a good idea as it will provide a real opportunity to specialise in working with higher risk individuals and protecting the public.

Strongly Agree	Agree	Neither Agree nor Disagree	Disagree	Strongly Disagree
○	○	○	○	○

21. There are bound to be problems of communication between the CRCs and the NPS that will cause problems in individual cases.

Strongly Agree	Agree	Neither Agree nor Disagree	Disagree	Strongly Disagree
○	○	○	○	○

Index

A

accountability 79, 85, 87
aims and objectives of the service
  behavioural change 16, 18, 19, 25,
    27–8, 42, 54–9, 102–3
  desistance 20, 33, 57, 103
  enforcement 26, 29, 31, 49, 56
  historically 7–8, 24–6
  public protection 23, 24, 29–30,
    54–6, 64, 70
  and reasons for joining 16–22
  rehabilitation 7, 8, 9, 24, 25, 45–6,
    54–7, 64, 66, 102
  respondents' views 53–60, 77–8,
    102–3
  in *Transforming Rehabilitation*
    10–11, 54
  see also expectations of the service;
    values
America 87–8
Annison, J. 22, 40
Ashworth, A. 3
assessment systems (OASys) 45, 53,
  64, 72
attitudinal data 116–26
autonomy, loss of 66–7

B

behavioural change 16, 18, 19, 25,
  27–8, 42, 54–9, 102–3
blog ('Jim Brown') 96, 99
Blunkett, David 24

Bourdieu, P. 97–8
Building Better Relationships
  (BBR) 46
bureaucracy 43, 46, 48–9, 63, 66–7
Burke, L. 12
Burnett, R. 41

C

career opportunities 45, 51–3
Carter Report 9
change, and organisations 98–9
Cheliotis, L.K. 8
Chief Inspector of Probation 97
civil service 66–7, 76–7
Clare, R. 103
Clarke, K. 9, 101
Coalition government (2010) 9, 95
cognitive behaviourism 46, 57
Collett, S. 56–7
commissioning structure 10–11
communication issues 65–6, 71–4,
  77
Community Rehabilitation
  Companies (CRCs)
  agendas of 77–8
  and commissioning structures
    10–11
  and communication with NPS 65,
    71–4, 77
  competition between 73
  and division of labour with NPS
    52, 62–6

and effective supervision 12, 97
and employment protection/
  security 11, 52
and governance 11–13
legitimacy of staff 77
ownership arrangements 1, 11–13
and professional status 52
and relationship with NPS 10,
  61–6, 69–78
and short term prisoners 97
staff qualifications/training 10,
  51–2, 59, 76–7, 80
staffing of 10, 11, 51–2, 59, 75–7
status of 52, 74–7
and values 33, 77–8, 103–4
see also privatisation
competition 72–3, 81, 101
compliance, and legitimacy 82, 83,
  89–90, 97, 102
Conservative government 7
CRCs see Community
  Rehabilitation Companies
Crewe, B. 36, 85, 91–2, 102
Criminal Justice Act (1991) 7, 23–4

D

Deering, J. 25–6, 68, 101
desistance 20, 33, 57, 103
division of labour (NPS and CRCs)
  62–6

E

electronic monitoring 69, 83
employment protection/security
  11, 52–3
enforcement 26, 29, 31, 49, 56
expectations of the service 39–48
 negative comments 43–7
 positive comments 42–3
 see also values

F

Facebook 96
Farrow, K. 40–1

feminisation of service 22–3
field, organisational 98
future scenarios 97–100

G

G4S 68, 102
gender differences, and agreed set of
  values 22–3

H

habitus 98–9
Her Majesty's Inspectorate of
  Probation report 72
high-risk offenders
 and communication 73
 and CRC staff 52, 78
 and NPS staff 62–3, 64–5, 78
 and senior managers 32
Hucklesby, A. 69, 83

I

idealised service 78–81
information
 loss of 65, 71
 sharing 65–6, 71–4
IT systems 48, 72

J

Jackson, J. 82–3
job satisfaction 39–47, 52–3, 64
job security 11, 52–3

K

Kinman, G. 39–40

L

Labour Government (1997) 8, 9,
  24
leadership see management
legitimacy
 and compliance 82, 83, 89–90,
  97, 102

of CRC staff 77
external 86, 87
internal 82–3, 87–8, 90, 102
and privatisation 82–91, 102
and quality of work 83–5, 89–92
Liebling, A. 36, 85, 91–2, 102

M

management
criticisms of 35–7, 44, 48
at odds with practitioners 34–7,
100
and values 31–2, 34–6
and views on quality 98
Managing Offenders, reducing crime 9
marketisation 9, 33, 85, 101, 103
see also privatisation
Mawby, R.C. 23, 26, 41
McNeill, F. 25, 83
Multi-Agency Public Protection
Arrangements (MAPPA) 17, 63

N

Napo 4–5, 11, 25, 31, 70, 72
National Offender Management
Service (NOMS) 9, 20, 41, 70, 80
National Probation Service for
England and Wales 8, 10, 24
National Probation Service (NPS)
agendas of 77–8
as civil service 66–7, 76–7
and communication with CRCs
65, 71–4, 77
and division of labour with CRCs
52, 61–6
and employment protection/
security 11
relationship with CRCs 10, 61–6,
69–78
staff qualifications 76
staffing of 10, 23, 52, 63, 76
views on working for 62–78
National Standards 7, 24, 49

O

OASys (Offender Assessment
System) 45, 53, 64, 72
objectives of service *see* aims and
objectives of the service
Offender Management Act (2007)
9, 10
Offender Rehabilitation Act (2014)
10, 97
On Probation (blog) 96, 99
organisational change 97–8
organisational field 98

P

partnership work 80–1
Payment by Results (PbR) 10–11,
77
penal theory 12
prison service 11, 39–40, 76, 85,
91–2
privatisation
background to 8–9
and commissioning structures
10–11
and electronic monitoring 69, 83
and ideal role of private sector
78–9, 81
and legitimacy 82–91, 102
and Offender Management Act
(2007) 9
and ownership arrangements of
CRCs 1, 11–13
and prison system 11, 76, 85, 91–2
profit from crime 12, 68, 77–8, 81,
82, 85, 86–9, 101–2
public debate on 95–97
views on 11, 21, 48, 51, 52, 68–9,
77–9, 81, 84–92, 101–2
see also Community Rehabilitation
Companies (CRCs)
Probation Institute 104
Probation of Offenders Act (1907)
23
probation orders 7, 23–4

Probation Service, reasons for joining 16–22, 100
Probation Service history 7–9
Probation Trusts 4, 9, 62, 67, 81
public debate (on probation) 95–7
public protection 23, 24, 29–30, 54–6, 64, 70
purpose of service *see* aims and objectives of the service

Q

qualifications 6, 21, 22, 24, 51, 59, 76–7

R

Raynor, P. 7, 56
rehabilitation
concept of 2–4, 54, 83
as purpose of the service 7, 8, 9, 24, 25, 45–6, 54–7, 64, 66, 102
as reason for joining probation service 16, 18, 19
and *Transforming Rehabilitation* 3–4, 24, 54
under pressure 31, 32
as value of the service 25, 27–30
relationship with offenders 2–3, 12, 23, 33, 58–9, 83, 84
respondent demographics 5–6, 127–8
risk assessment/management
and high-risk offenders 32, 52, 62–5, 73, 78
and lack of communication with CRCs 65, 73–4
and NPS staff 10, 62–5, 77–8
as purpose of the service 54–6, 102
as reason for joining service 18
as value of the service 26, 29–30
Roberts, J. 3
Robinson, G. 3, 25, 41, 55, 83, 98–9

role of the service *see* aims and objectives of the service

S

security of employment 11, 52–3
senior management *see* management
Serco 68, 102
SFOs (serious further offences) 63, 65, 66, 73, 74
short-term prisoners 10, 35, 97, 100
social media 96, 97, 99
Sodexo Justice Services 97
staff *see* workforce
staff shortages 63, 72
Staff Transfer Scheme 11
Sunshine, J. 82
supervision
and CRCs 12, 97
and high-risk offenders 62–4
in an ideal world 78–81
management vs practitioner views 34–5
within NPS 62–3, 64
as purpose of the service 54
and quality of the service 98–9
and relationship with offenders 2–3, 12, 23, 33, 58–9, 83, 84
of short-term prisoners 10, 34–5, 97
and *Transforming Rehabilitation* 10, 12, 62–3
see also aims and objectives of the service; Community Rehabilitation Companies (CRCs); expectations of the service; National Probation Service (NPS); privatisation
survey 4–6
analysis methods 6
attitudinal data 116–26
full survey 129–43
number of respondents 4

respondent demographics 5–6, 127–8

T

third sector 13, 78–9, 81, 88, 89, 90
training 10, 24, 59, 80, 89
Transforming Rehabilitation (TR)
 content of 3–4, 10–12, 54, 62
 early impact of 72–3
 lack of information on 62
 and penal theory 12
 and public debate 95–7
 and rehabilitation 3–4, 24, 54
 respondents' views on 51–3, 69–70, 89, 92
 unknowable outcomes of 97–9
 see also Community Rehabilitation Companies (CRCs); National Probation Service (NPS); privatisation
Tyler, T. 82

U

United States 87–8

V

values
 agreed set of 22–30, 44
 and expectations of the service 39–48
 holding on to 103–4
 management vs practitioners 34–7
 under pressure 30–4, 49–51
 reasons for decline 48–53

W

Williams, B. 24–5
workforce
 breakdown of relationships 71
 career progression of 45, 51–3
 communication issues 65–6, 71–4, 77
 and division of labour 62–6

employment protection/security of 11, 52–3
loss of staff 70, 76–7
management and practitioners at odds 34–7
qualifications of 6, 21, 22, 24, 51, 59, 76–7
reasons for joining service 16–22, 100
staff shortages 63, 72
Staff Transfer Scheme 11
them and us mentality 74–7
training of 10, 24, 59, 80, 89
 see also Community Rehabilitation Companies (CRCs); National Probation Service (NPS)
workload, and division of labour 62–6
Worrall, A. 23, 26, 41

Z

Zedner, L. 45–6